HARVEST
of
GRIEF

D0873338

HARVEST

OF

GRIEF

Grasshopper Plagues
and Public Assistance in
Minnesota, 1873–78

ANNETTE ATKINS

"We were eaten up by speculators, politicians, now
grasshoppers, the people said. Hoppers eat everything but the mortgage."
MERIDEL LE SUEUR
North Star Country

MINNESOTA HISTORICAL SOCIETY PRESS

2004 reprint of 1984 edition

The frontispiece and cover are from a lithograph made of a sketch by Howard Purcell, 1874, in the possesssion of the author. The pictures of the hopper-dozers and the 1876 map of the United States are from the United States Dept. of the Interior, Geological Survey, *Report of the Entomological Commission for 1877* (Washington, D.C., 1878). All others are in the collections of the Minnesota Historical Society.

Published with funds provided to the Minnesota Historical Society Public Affairs Center by the Northwest Area Foundation, St. Paul, Minnesota.

www.mnhs.org/mhspress

The Minnesota Historical Society Press is a member of the Association of American University Presses.

MANUFACTURED IN THE UNITED STATES OF AMERICA

International Standard Book Number 0-87351-479-3

Library of Congress Cataloging-in-Publication Data
Atkins, Annette, 1950–
    Harvest of grief/
    Bibliography: p.
    Includes index.
    1. Agriculture and State—Minnesota—History—19th century.
    2. Agriculture—Economic aspects—Minnesota—History—19th century.
    3. Disaster relief—Minnesota—History—19th century.
    4. Rocky Mountain locust—Minnesota—History—19th century.
    I. Title
    HD1775.M6A78   338.1'8776   84-10855

For Bart

Contents

Illustrations

Preface

My dad grew up on a farm near Lennox, South Dakota. During the dust bowl years of the 1930s he stayed out of high school for a year to help his family work a place that they did not even own. This hard year convinced him to find his future away from the farm. And when he left for college he turned toward the city, where he has stayed. He still enjoys gardening and grows great tomatoes, but he has never regretted his decision. The rewards of farming were too small, he remembers, and the threats too great. But he was the only boy in his family to leave.

While visiting my parents several years ago, I attended a reunion of my father's family. The men sat around talking about crops and weather and that year's prospects. My uncles and their sons were worried. If rain did not come soon, they would need to plow their crops under. I was only on the periphery of this conversation, partly because I was a "kid" in an adult's world, a "townie" listening to discussion of a rural subject, a woman in a man's domain. But I paid attention. And the conversation stuck with me.

Several days later I awoke early to hear my mother closing the bedroom windows against the pounding rain. For most of that morning I stood at the front door and watched the rain. By mid-morning the hail came, small and steady. I thought about my uncles and aunts, my cousins, their neighbors, their friends. I wondered whether they too were standing at their front doors watching, calculating, planning, worrying. Then I speculated on how often they had stood like this seeing their crops destroyed and their livelihood threatened. And I thought about the generations of farm people who had watched the weather and witnessed the loss of their crops. Finally, I wondered how they could bear it. How can farm people stay on the land and face these threats year after year?

I know that others of us face threats — students can fail exams and flunk out of school; we can be deprived of our jobs by retrenchment or technological changes; we can lose our houses to fire or our

1

belongings to theft. We can break our legs or get hurt in car accidents. Each of these could pose a serious threat, but each seems more remote, less immediately probable, less constant and damaging than the weather. Besides, we can study harder, change schools, get alternate job training. And the threat of fire or theft (particularly in rural Minnesota where I live) seems too remote to worry about much. But farmers cannot simply work harder or trick themselves by saying, "It can't happen to me." It can happen to them and it does.

In the middle 1870s, throughout the Upper Midwest, particularly in Minnesota, Dakota Territory, Iowa, Nebraska, Kansas, Missouri, and Manitoba, thousands of farm people lost all or part of their crops to Rocky Mountain locusts, commonly called grasshoppers. In some areas, for as long as five consecutive years, the grasshoppers took all they wanted and left only stubble behind. Year after year the crops failed, and year after year farm people either stood and watched or fought back with useless tools.

My study of these plagues could have taken several directions. John T. Schlebecker, in his 1953 article, "Grasshoppers in American Agricultural History," noted that while historians have examined how the environment shaped the frontier experience, we have largely ignored the "lowly, despicable grasshopper." He maintained that a closer study of the various infestations would reveal that they had had a profound impact on farmers. He suggested, for example, that the attacks forced greater emphasis on livestock raising and crop diversification. More important, he argued, historians might find a causal connection between grasshopper problems and the rise of agrarian unrest at the end of the nineteenth century.[1]

My own research suggests that his hunches are at least partially correct. Some farmers did alter their cropping patterns. They did put in more and different crops in an attempt to find one that was grasshopper resistant or, at least, to find a product that would survive the depredations. Farmers may also have raised fewer chickens, as eggs produced by chickens that had fed on grasshoppers proved inedible. These new practices did not, however, survive long after the plagues had ended.

A possible connection between the plagues and politics is even more fascinating and I, with Schlebecker, suspect a study of this aspect would bear fruit. During the hard times of the 1870s, farmers in the Midwest received some assistance from the federal government, albeit less than some farmers (and politicians) wanted. Nonetheless, the government proved to be helpful, even if it did not display the New Deal generosity of the next century.

If the farmers of the 1870s viewed this assistance as valuable, they could have been disappointed and angry when later calls for help went unheeded. When, in the late 1880s and 1890s, hard times returned in the form of drought and economic depression, the government turned a less sympathetic ear. And it seemed, too, that the American people proved to be less interested in agricultural troubles, facing as they were their own depression (more serious than that of the 1870s) and the dislocations of industrialization and urbanization. The farmers, once accustomed to assistance, may have assumed that the government, and individuals, would again help. When there was no response, farmers possibly felt cheated and even betrayed by a government and a people who had aided them before.

This study could also have followed up other questions — how did governments in the various states and territories respond to the threat that the grasshoppers posed? How many bushels of grain were left unharvested that might have been saved? How did this number compare with losses of other times, other places? How were these plagues like others? How did they differ? I could have asked when the first infestations appeared and why. And, the question most asked by friends: Why don't we have grasshopper plagues today?

These problems continued to pique my interest and set me thinking about the consequences and implications of attacks by the "lowly and despicable" grasshopper. But I chose a different approach. My uncles do not talk much and they give brief answers to my questions about why they stay on the farm in the face of constant trouble. So, I chose a direction that would help me understand my uncles and their parents and their parents and their parents.

My uncles do not tell me, and the people of the 1870s cannot, why they stayed on the farm, but I can look at personal correspondence, newspapers, and county and state records. Where I cannot find answers about individuals I can find them about groups. The question of why people stayed led me immediately to that of what choices they had. How was it possible for them to stay? Did they ask for aid? Whom did they ask? What help did they get? Did assistance come with strings attached? What strings?

The more I investigated, the more surprised I was by what I found. I expected to learn, for example, that Minnesotans would draw a clear line between, on one side, farmers who needed help for

3

reasons beyond their control — natural disasters — and, on the other side, paupers who, in the nineteenth century, were often blamed for their condition. Normally — if anything can be normal in a disaster — sufferers escape the criticisms of those unsympathetic to public assistance; clearly, victims of tornadoes or floods cannot be held accountable for their plight. Even the strictest nineteenth-century moralist or Social Darwinist could not charge these sufferers with lapses of morality or of initiative. Consequently, I expected that expressions of public sympathy or generosity would be offered without fear of creating a permanent class of the needy. I particularly anticipated that few Minnesotans would worry about the moral fiber of these people, who, after all, were farmers. How could Americans question the moral values of the salt of the earth?

Yet, soon, especially during the administration of Governor John S. Pillsbury, plague victims became categorized as the poor, as mendicants. Many public officials treated them with a suspicion bordering on contempt, a characteristic of poor-relief administration.

This work does not claim to be a complete history of the midwestern grasshopper plagues of the 1870s. It studies the response to the plagues personally, locally, and at state and national levels. This approach provides an occasion for analyzing social welfare issues, for understanding attitudes, and for examining the relationship between farm people and their government.

I have concentrated on the experience in a single geographical section — Minnesota. The farm people in this state during the 1870s did not differ significantly from those elsewhere in the Midwest. Some had taken up residence later than those in Iowa or earlier than those in Dakota Territory, but the context in which they made their decisions did not vary much from place to place. The governmental structures of midwestern states and territories deviated little from one to another, and the laws, particularly those governing the care and treatment of the poor, were similar.

Focusing on one state enabled me to carry the story through the period, to trace changes within a relatively stable environment. Moreover, concentration made possible the depth that inclusiveness mitigated against. My point is not that Minnesota is more important than other areas, but that the response in this state offers one story that can be reported and analyzed and has implications and patterns beyond this particular locale.

4

Only the roles of the churches and the foreign language press get short shrift. The churches were not included because my most careful searching of the available records yielded almost nothing. If pastors, priests, and church groups offered aid to the needy, they left no mention in parish papers or in the state records. My lack of sufficient facility in the languages, rather than any absence of interest or attention, accounts for the omission of the foreign language newspapers.

A post-New Deal author writing about a pre-New Deal age faces the temptation to apply in reverse modern attitudes about the role of government. People in the 1980s are so accustomed to big government that we must regularly remind ourselves that governments of the nineteenth century conceived of their function differently and acted differently. I confess my own ideological approval of official assistance. Yet, a careful and fair reading of nineteenth-century records suggests that the New Deal did not entirely redirect public attitudes about the government's role, although it did make lawmakers more responsive to requests for help. The hundreds of letters written by individual farm people to Governors Cushman K. Davis and John S. Pillsbury during the 1870s asking, begging, pleading for help, suggest at least that these people believed that the state should come to their assistance. Whether or not these farm people thought the state had an obligation to assist them, they did ask. Whether or not these people had an articulated ideology that expressed a New Deal-like set of attitudes, they did turn for help to their local officials, their legislators, their governors. Where I am critical of the state government in general or Governor Pillsbury in particular, I draw my criticism from the frustrated expectations of the farmers, not simply from my application of anachronistic, latter-day values. People ask for help from those whom they expect or at least hope will come to their rescue.

If this book does not provide a complete history of the depredations and the implications of the plagues, it does aspire to tell as full a story as possible of how a specific group of people reacted to the repeated loss of their crops over several years. It tells of how more prosperous farmers and townspeople, private citizens and public officials, responded to hard-working, disaster-hit human beings in need.

5

This book bears the name of one author but should list dozens of collaborators — friends, colleagues, teachers, archivists, editors — who made the project possible, better, and enjoyable. I will mention only a few of them.

My friends Carol Summers, Dale Sorenson, Joyce Goldberg, Robert Barrows, Larry and Sally Hogan, Emil Pocock, and Robert Spaeth learned more about grasshoppers than they ever wanted and offered in exchange suggestions, enthusiasm, and true companionship. Clarke Chambers improved my thinking, writing, and morale. Arthur Rye was one of my best cheerleaders but did not live to see the results of his encouragement. Janet McNew, Linda Hansen, Joan Steck, and Jack Farley helped me teach and write at the same time.

Lynda Fish and Pamela Schrader typed like crazy and did those many things that make authors' lives easier. I owe them many, many thanks and the promise that they will never type another word about grasshoppers and farmers.

My teachers M. Jeanne Peterson, Otto Pflanze, Warren Gardner, Joseph Amato, Maynard Brass, David Nass, and Duane Leach taught me how to think and write historically. Martin Ridge originally suggested the topic and sat with Robert Gunderson and Paula Hudis on my dissertation committee. Walter Nugent chaired that committee and continues to inspire me by his commitment to scholarship and his active interest in ideas.

The staff of the Minnesota Historical Society, particularly Dallas Lindgren, Ruth Bauer, and Ruby Shields, guided me through their rich collections with patience and friendliness. Byrum Zurn and the Chippewa County Courthouse staff even dusted off century-old boxes in the courthouse basement. Mildred Throne, curator of the Martin County Historical Society, opened the records and her house to me during my stay in Fairmont.

Sally Rubinstein is the kind of editor we all hope to find. She copy edited, checked notes, and smoothed the manuscript. Kindly and generously she walked me through the process of finishing and publishing a book.

My parents Elizabeth and Robert Atkins always lent a hand (and a dollar) when I most needed it. My husband Barton Sutter did not darn my socks or type the manuscript, but he did tease, joke, listen, read, encourage, needle, and appreciate.

1

A Value System Threatened

To create the atmosphere for a play, a playwright provides stage directions to set the scene. These directions describe the arrangement of furniture, the landscape, and the background. They specify the posture and placement of the actors at the moment when the curtain goes up. These instructions aim to create the appropriate setting for developing the story. The setting and the atmosphere perform no less an important role in telling a historical story.

The actors in this account of the grasshopper plagues of the 1870s made individual, personal decisions based on their own experiences and circumstances. Farm people who had money, stability, generous friends and relatives, or other sources of income could behave differently from those who hung on while waiting for their next crop and ate mostly what they had preserved from their gardens. The actions and decisions of the state legislator from the city of Minneapolis may have differed from those of a county commissioner in Martin County.

Individuals, however, exist within a cultural context that influences their specific attitudes, decisions, and behavior. The actors in this play found themselves on a particular stage at a particular time where certain scripts were more likely than others. Among the variety of reactions to the grasshopper plagues we do not, for example, find people dancing in the fields or making animal sacrifices to appease the gods of insects — actions that might be suitable to another time and place. In the 1870s they asked the government for help. They built "hopperdozers" or prayed, pledging to build chapels if the scourge were lifted. The decision to offer a chapel rather than an animal sacrifice is related to culture.

Culture, as defined by anthropologists, constitutes the set of mental categories through which individuals in a given society structure their understanding of the world. As Kai Erikson stated, "Cultural forms help determine how people will think and act and feel . . . [and] imagine." The culture of the United States shaped the reactions to grasshoppers; it influenced the settlers' decisions about whether to ask for assistance, and how and from whom. Views held in the larger society about the necessity of extending aid, and how and by whom, also derived from the national culture. These decisions and ideas did not occur suddenly, simply in reaction to a particular series of events. Nor did they take place in a Midwest detached from the rest of the United States. But they did occur in an America that honored certain ideals and paid homage to certain values.[1]

While each society holds an array of beliefs and ideas, anthropologists suggest that to understand a given society we must identify "core" values, those central to the group's definition of itself. These core values provoke strong emotion, either negative or positive, and form the criteria by which an individual is rewarded or punished. As long as these values form a consistent and mutually reinforcing system, the culture remains strong and viable. If, however, certain values become incompatible with others, the resulting conflict is labeled in psychological literature as "cognitive dissonance." Dissonance creates tension that cannot be sustained indefinitely if the culture is to survive. The intensity of the conflict reflects the relative importance of the ideas that have become incompatible.[2]

In nineteenth-century America, two particular core values powerfully influenced both group and individual response to the plight of the Midwest's destitute settlers: the belief that farmers constituted America's chosen people; the commitment to the work ethic. By mid-century, however, two other values were gaining strength: "modernization" and money. As they stood arrayed against the former two, they produced cultural cognitive dissonance.

Of the thousands of migrants who set their faces westward and the thousands among them who made their living from the soil, probably only a few had read Thomas Jefferson's *Notes on the State of Virginia*; but most probably knew and shared his sentiments. "Those who labour in the earth," Jefferson wrote, "are the chosen people of God, if ever he had a chosen people, whose breasts he has made his peculiar deposit for substantial and genuine virtue." Alexander Hamilton and a few other Federalists may have disagreed, but even they would not have denied that such words represented and reflected a dominant strain in American culture. In fact, the high emotional pitch of the disagreement between Jefferson and Hamilton over the agricultural or industrial future of the United States offers evidence of the centrality and significance of agrarianism as a value.[3]

The farmer breaking the virgin soil symbolized what was good in Americans as a people — independence, industry, determination, initiative. The farmers' nobility and central place in American culture were touted in newspapers, magazines, preachers' sermons, novels, McGuffey's readers, and politicians' rhetoric. Moreover, the independent yeomen upheld family and community, and guaranteed stability, continuity, and order.

Farmers stood surrounded by family (another American value). Father, mother, and children formed a co-operative, contented working team. The farmer moved westward with his "Madonna of the Plains" to create civilization out of chaos. In these people reposed all that was good and wholesome in American society.

The second core value honored by Americans has come to be called the work ethic. It embodied a set of ideas that, according to historian Daniel T. Rodgers, placed labor at "the core of the moral life." To work was good; not to work was bad. The industrious man or woman was, by definition, a moral person. If in an earlier time work brought religious rewards, in the nineteenth century it brought (or bought) the good life. Work carried the promise of success, of God's blessing, and of prosperity. Matthew Hale Smith sermonized in 1873, "Industry, honesty, perseverance, sticking to one thing, invariably lead to success." He did not say "should," or "might," but "invariably." The work ethic also included the idea that individuals controlled their future and their destiny. No battle was too great, no obstacle too high to prevent an industrious person from reaching a set goal. Whether Americans paid only lip service or had a real commitment to these values became a moot point as other values became increasingly visible, powerful, and attractive.[4]

Industrialists, entrepreneurs, and big businessmen competed with farmers for cultural significance. Capitalists stood for different values — for progress, modernization, growth, and expansion — based on cash instead of land. They offered another kind of individualism and a new vision of America, both of which encompassed money, power, and sophistication. In comparison, farmers often appeared to be "hicks" and bumpkins, old fashioned and stodgy. Industrialists created commercial empires and amassed great fortunes. The names of Carnegie, Morgan, Hill, Vanderbilt, and Rockefeller became associated with an increasingly desirable set of American values.

How could Americans honor such different ideals? How could they venerate, at one and the same time, the family farmer and the businessman whose work and ambition precluded a substantial family life? How could a farmer's 160 acres compete in the public imagination with a booming factory or a transcontinental railroad? And, how could the farmer's plowed furrows and snug barn compare with the industrialist's personal wealth? What farmer could endow a public library or a university or a museum? Did work indicate worth and value, or did money?

Moreover, in the mid- to late-nineteenth century, farmers faced a series of nearly crushing difficulties while industrialists prospered. It became harder and harder for the society to honor farmers as unrivaled heroes and the only "true" Americans when farming did not bring unparalleled rewards, when towns grew too fast and young women and men abandoned the farms and rushed to the cities. Industry was simply becoming too powerful, influential, and public to take second place in American values for long.

Work itself as a value seemed also to be under siege, or at least in serious ideological trouble. Any American could identify dozens of people who worked hard but went unrewarded: the blacksmith who labored all his life and died not much better off than when he started; the widow who slaved night and day and never quite got ahead; the storekeeper whose income rose and fell with the vicissitudes of his neighbors, not with the number of hours he logged. Examples were endless and were even more obvious in urban America. Laborers — men, women, and children — toiled endlessly in the factories. Not only did they fail to get rich, they did not even get on their feet.

Americans could have identified another flaw in the work ethic — people who did not seem to work hard received rewards and became successful. Ragged Dick, a typical Horatio Alger hero, got rich not through hard work but through quick wit, accident, luck, being in the right place at the right time, and marrying right. Good fortune made for good breaks and good breaks made for better fortunes. Alger rarely depicted his heroes doing any hard work. Bankers, railroad owners, people who invested well did not seem to work much either, yet they lived comfortably and well. John D. Rockefeller retired while in his fifties so that he could carry on his philanthropy. James Vanderbilt built a large and imposing house in New

York City to which he returned for rest at the end of the day — a day shorter and a rest longer than that afforded the day laborer in most local factories.[5]

Thus, in the nineteenth century, Americans faced a conflict between ideas and practice, between values and behavior. They valued farmers and work, yet more seriously admired industrialists and money. They measured success by money and by values that left most farmers "unsuccessful" and work without its promised rewards. Somehow, Americans had to resolve this ideological conflict; they had to bring back into line their values or their behavior.

The adjustment that Americans made in the work ethic had serious consequences for the treatment of the poor. Instead of accepting the evidence that work did not guarantee success, Americans looked at those without money and decided that since they lacked money they must not be successful. And, if they were not successful they must not have worked hard enough. Where once work itself had signified success, in mid-nineteenth-century America an accumulation of money indicated it. Money, not work, became proof of the moral life, but Americans still talked about the "work" ethic. As Americans came to measure worth by money, they measured lack of worth by lack of money. The poor never received generous and compassionate treatment, but rarely in the country's history were they treated less kindly and compassionately than in the last third of the nineteenth century.

If David Rothman is correct, the poor of colonial America received care rather routinely. Following Elizabethan Poor Law precedent and tradition, local governments assumed responsibility for the needy when individual efforts proved inadequate. In the early nineteenth century, social reformers worried that relief encouraged destitution by rewarding the pauper. Economic reformers criticized the costs of the system. These worries led to what Rothman called "the discovery of the asylum." Reformers replaced "outdoor" relief — that received at home — with poorhouses to provide "indoor" relief, directly supervised by a public overseer. While unpleasant, the poorhouses and poor farms were neither vicious nor cruel.[6]

"True nastiness," as Clarke A. Chambers termed it, began to characterize public administration of relief "after the 1840s with the coming of the Irish, who were so different from the host society, presumably. . . ." Not only the Irish immigrant but also the rise of the new money ethic provoked this response. Because a slim wallet

11

indicated a short supply of American virtues, the poor, whether immigrant or native born, stood accused of possessing a weakened moral fiber.[7]

These needy did not merit public aid; instead, they needed moral suasion and advice. All that was necessary, the reformers believed, was to train the poor in "American" values and behavior, particularly work, sobriety, independence, and other "Horatio Alger" and Yankee habits. Self-righteousness and outrage characterized the administration of public and private charity at the end of the nineteenth century. In pursuit of the best interests of the poor, the charitable too often offered only harsh words and a cold hand.

Clearly Americans had never undervalued money nor despised wealthy merchants, planters, and businessmen. The Puritans, among others, placed high social, cultural, and religious emphasis on money and property. In fact, prosperity could indicate God's favor and the blessed state of an individual's soul. Yet, until the late nineteenth century, Americans held values, including those of work and agrarianism, that balanced and limited the emphasis on money. Until industrialization and urbanization increased substantially, until the number of people engaged in farming declined, money itself did not define or stand for success, achievement, and worth. But, in the late-nineteenth century the disjunction and incompatibility increased between the ideological value of farmers and their relative lack of success and wealth. The cognitive dissonance in American culture was strong, pervasive, and confusing.

As the curtain goes up on the 1870s, we see farmers fighting for their place in American culture and society. The notion of their nobility is still held but is being sorely tested and will not survive the century intact. The money ethic is supplanting the work ethic as the indicator of worth and values. Americans continue to speak of the work ethic and live with the contradictions.

When grasshoppers invaded Minnesota in the 1870s, they not only left many farm families in acute need but also brought America's incompatible values into direct conflict. The farmers, in whom reposed much of what Americans said they valued and honored, had become poor. Settlers worked hard, but were still in need. Were they paupers? Did they deserve charity? Would farmers, too, be blamed for their poverty? These questions surfaced when a dark rustling cloud, making buzzing and snipping sounds, appeared on Minnesota's western horizon in June 1873.

2

Plague: The Grasshoppers Arrive

"Farming always has been a risky, uncertain, and sometimes heart-breaking business," wrote historian Gilbert C. Fite, "but pioneer settlers in the 1870s on the upper midwest and central prairie frontier were confronted with an unusual series of hardships." This series included hail and blizzards, prairie fires and drought, low prices, high interest rates, and excessive railroad rates. The most intense and prolonged hardships, however, resulted from consecutive years of grasshopper plagues.[1]

In 1873 grasshoppers invaded a swath of territory from northern Colorado and southern Wyoming eastward through Nebraska and Dakota Territory, and across northern Iowa and southern and central Minnesota. They returned annually, 1874–77, and appeared also in parts of Texas, Arkansas, Indian Territory (Oklahoma), Missouri, Kansas, Idaho, Montana, Utah, New Mexico, Nevada, Washington, Oregon, and the Canadian provinces of Manitoba, Alberta, and Saskatchewan.[2]

The United States Entomological Commission attempted in 1878 to estimate the damage occasioned by the successive grasshopper plagues. To determine the cost for 1874, which the commissioners called the "most disastrous" year, they calculated what would have been the crop yield in 1874, based on the yields of previous years and the number of acres under cultivation. They compared those figures to the actual yields, subtracted to take account of the dry conditions that also affected the crops, and determined a rough dollar amount for the destruction in Iowa, Missouri, Kansas, and Nebraska: $56 million. Moreover, the commissioners declared, this figure did not come close to accounting for the real damage to the people and the states. "The check to business, improvements, and the various industrial enterprises," they wrote, "the effect these visitations have of

13

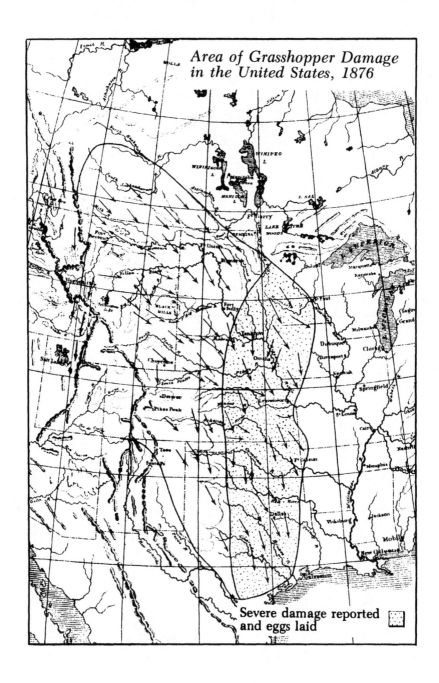

Area of Grasshopper Damage
in the United States, 1876

Severe damage reported
and eggs laid

stopping immigration and driving away capital, bring upon these new States a greater loss than that sustained by the crops." Considering these secondary effects, the commissioners suggested that a figure of $100 million more closely conveyed the actual damage in 1874.

In making these estimates, the commissioners lacked information about the number of acres under cultivation, the number damaged, and the number affected by other problems that beset agriculture. For the years besides 1874 the commissioners offered only a few estimates, these with even less precision. The nearest they came to a general figure was this statement: "It is fair to presume that in the entire locust-visited area, during these years, the total loss would fall but little, if any, short of $200,000,000."[3]

The cause of the damage was a small, olive-brown insect formally identified as the *Caloptenus Spretus* and called "Rocky Mountain locust" by entomologists. The term locust, from the Latin "locus ustus" meaning "burnt place," accurately and graphically described the landscape after an infestation. Settlers stuck with "grasshoppers."

The grasshoppers did their damage in two phases. Initially they swept out of the foothills of the Rocky Mountains, looking for food. The hungry pests could, according to a leading contemporary entomologist, "sweep a field quicker than would a whole herd of hungry steers." Other scientists described the Rocky Mountain locust as a "terrible engine of destruction." Virtually all vegetation — with the possible exception of tomatoes, castor beans, and raspberries — was vulnerable. The grasshoppers had a particular taste for grains, cereals, and clothing hanging out to dry.

The losses during this first phase were bad enough, but a greater threat remained. The laying season lasted about six weeks, and a mature, healthy female could lay four to six pods of twenty-eight eggs each. The female deposited her eggs in the ground about an inch below the surface — safe from most predators — usually in loosely cultivated fields. The eggs remained dormant until spring and hatched about the time the wheat began to sprout. The fledgling grasshoppers, wingless for six to eight weeks, could only crawl to satisfy their voracious appetites. They feasted on tender young vegetation. After the young developed wings, the cycle then began anew.

The people of these states and territories variously felt the effects of the invasions. Some farms escaped damage altogether or suffered minimally or were hurt only once or twice. Other people lost every-

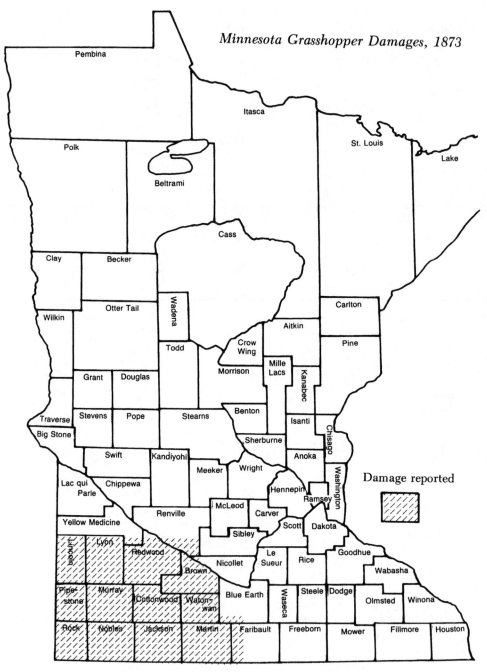

Minnesota Grasshopper Damages, 1873

Damage reported

thing, again and again. Thus, no clear-cut pattern existed; the damage varied from crop to crop, from farm to farm, from place to place, and from year to year. This account of the plagues focuses on Minnesota, but the conditions were prevalent throughout the Midwest.

Most of the thousands who suffered from the plagues had no earlier experience with grasshoppers. In the first years of the invasions, people did not know what was happening or what to expect. But they recognized trouble. Novelist Ole E. Rølvaag described a scene that must have occurred throughout the Midwest. Rølvaag's hero, Per Hansa, and several neighbors stood together in the fields pleased with themselves and with their anticipated crop. "Never had the Lord sent finer weather for wheat to ripen in!" they all agreed. In a festive and exultant mood, one of the neighbors rejoiced, "Well, boys, in my opinion the Land of Canaan didn't have much on this country — no, I'm damned if it had!" In the midst of this gladness Per Hansa peered into the west and muttered to himself, "What in the devil!" What he saw he did not understand, but it "sent a nameless chill through his blood."[4]

Nonfictional accounts are no less dramatic. As one farmer recalled, "a large black cloud suddenly appeared high in the west from which came an ominous sound. The apparition moved directly toward us, its dark appearance became more and more terrifying and the sound changed to a deep hum. . . . We heard the buzzing; we saw the shining wings, the long bodies, the legs. The grasshoppers — the scourge of the prairie — were upon us." Another settler described his experience: "So many times I think of June 12, 1873. My younger brother and I were in school that day . . . and about two o'clock the great cloud of grasshoppers came down. We rushed out of school, and started home. We had to hold our hands over our faces to keep them from hitting us in our eyes." Other children, including Laura Ingalls Wilder, remembered being barefoot and unable to step anywhere without crushing the insects. Yet another eyewitness reported that the grasshoppers "moved as an army forty miles wide and a hundred and fifty miles long."[5]

When the grasshoppers alighted, they ate almost anything within sight. The reports range from a simple "they covered everything" and "They devoured the grass and crops of all description" to they "ate their crops except the potatoes." There were reports of ruined fruit trees, fork handles, and cloth items. The pests did not seem to bother

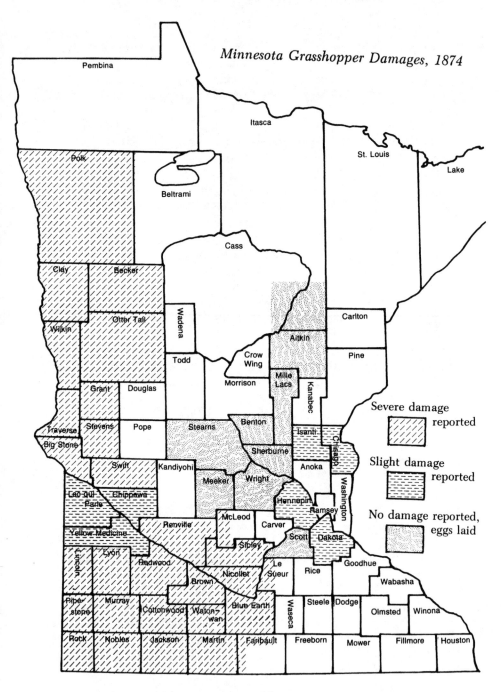

Minnesota Grasshopper Damages, 1874

Severe damage
reported

Slight damage
reported

No damage reported,
eggs laid

poultry or animals, but a few people said that the eggs and flesh of chickens that had fed on the insects were inedible.[6]

In many cases the grasshoppers appeared without any advance notice except for a darkening of the sun and a "strange whirring sound in the air" that one settler likened to "thousands of scissors cutting and snipping. . . ." Throughout the five years there were no reliable warnings. Not only was information difficult to obtain, but both printed and word-of-mouth predictions could be confusing. "There has [sic] been so many reports in circulation regarding the damage to crops by grasshoppers," the St. Paul Daily Pioneer reported in late July 1873, "that we hardly know what to depend upon."[7]

Even when warnings did circulate, farmers had good reasons to ignore them. The pests themselves defied easy predictions. Carried by the wind, they did minimal damage in some places, then moved on and wrought their worst elsewhere. So, while the newspaper reported that the "vanguard of the advancing army of grasshoppers" stretched a hundred miles long and ten miles wide, individual farmers witnessed sometimes sporadic infestations. One farmer, typical of many settlers, coupled his understanding of the pests with some wishful thinking. "The grasshoppers are 6 miles south west," he reported to his son, "Generally traveling a north east course, although somewhat irratic [sic] depending on the direction of the wind. If they continue on I think they will pass to the north of us." Later letters make clear that his prediction did not come true.[8]

Settlers might well have ignored forecasts for less practical reasons. Rarely did novelists give much attention to whether the farmers had been warned, but one novel suggests a likely set of responses to what alarms there were. Set in fictional Crockett County, but modeled closely on Martin County, Gentlemen From England, by Maud Hart Lovelace and Delos Lovelace, demonstrated how skillfully farmers could ignore the reports that did arrive. The hero, Richard Chalmers, had heard persistent rumors for over a month but "could not yield to grasshopper stories even a measure of alarm." The tales seemed too exaggerated. A "Vast ravenous army of insects . . . eating every growing thing and leaving desolation in its wake," he thought to himself; "Whoever had heard of such a visitation outside the pages of the Bible?"[9]

Chalmers, like many settlers, employed a hierarchy of defenses. First he ignored the stories, then denied them, and then told himself

19

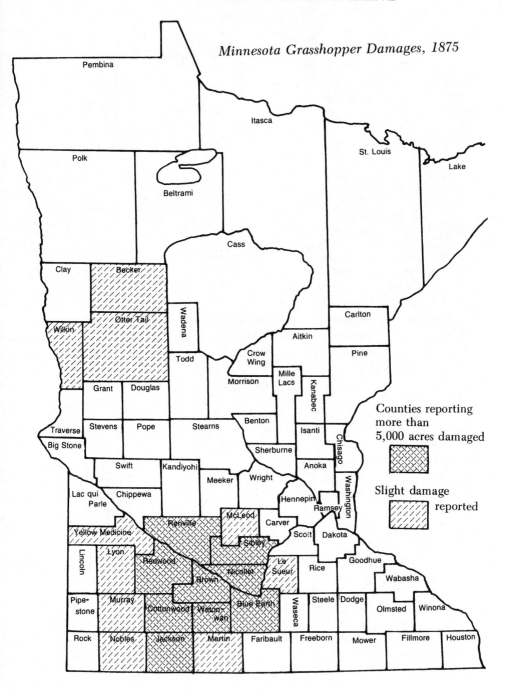

Minnesota Grasshopper Damages, 1875

Counties reporting
more than
5,000 acres damaged

Slight damage
reported

that even if the rumors were true, the pests could never reach Crockett County. Finally, even if the grasshoppers did come, he argued, they could not destroy whole fields. He was wrong.

Chalmers became only slightly alarmed when he heard that the insects had crossed into his county. For sport and to quell their slightly nagging fears, Chalmers and several neighbors rode west to see for themselves. They were "incredulously silent" when they first spotted the grasshopper cloud. Those outrageously exaggerated rumors had been neither outrageous nor exaggerated. Watching the creatures at work, Chalmers remembered a Bible passage: "The land is as the garden of Eden before them, and behind them a desolate wilderness." At last he believed.

During 1873, according to the state's statistician, "Minnesota was the banner state in the production of wheat . . . the yield on an equally large area exceeding that of any other state." In this context, wheat loss in the grasshopper infested areas was minimal. The pests accounted for the loss of over one-half million bushels — just over 2 percent — of the state's crop. In the eleven counties most severely hurt the wheat yield dropped by almost one-third. These counties also lost a quarter of their oats, half of their barley, and more than a third of their corn.[10]

At the end of the season the 1873 losses seemed to many like spilled milk — gone, with nothing to be done about it. The farmers could only hope for a better year in 1874. They knew that eggs had been laid but understood little of what that meant. In the spring of 1874 a Martin County farmer wrote his local newspaper, "the prospect never was and never could be better for crops of all kinds. Farmers [are] all fairly jubilant over their prospects and astonished to witness the power of this soil to force the growth of all kinds of vegetation. . . ." But soon the eggs began to hatch and the small, unfledged grasshoppers began their ravages throughout the eleven counties afflicted in 1873.[11]

By early June optimistic prospects for the year's crop had been dashed. Another Martin County resident reported, "the Western half of this County is entirely stripped of all crops . . . another week will finish the crops in the entire county." Several days later the wheat crop was declared "entirely destroyed." Similar news came from other areas. By the end of June the grasshoppers in Murray

Minnesota's Grain Crops Lost to Grasshoppers, 1873–77

YEAR	PERCENT OF TILLED LAND IN GRAIN CROPS	LOSSES IN BUSHELS (IN PERCENTAGE)				NUMBER OF COUNTIES DAMAGED
		Wheat	Oats	Corn	All Grain*	
1873	92.88	562,810 (2.09)**	213,576 (1.67)**	125,938 (1.91)**	5,277,874 (10.90)	11
1874	92.89	2,646,802 (9.96)	1,816,733 (14.21)	738,415 (9.14)	4,002,373 (7.09)	28
1875	93.16	2,024,972 (6.31)	1,127,780 (7.55)	790,981 (9.90)	7,151,095 (15.87)	19
1876	93.80	3,344,829 (15.70)	2,277,742 (17.73)	1,338,972 (14.94)	8,577,790 (13.26)	29
1877	93.77	4,957,538 (13.91)	1,757,370 (11.28)	1,665,993 (15.44)		20 †
TOTAL		13,536,951	7,193,201	4,660,299	—	

*wheat, oats, corn, barley, rye, buckwheat

**estimated

† an additional 11 counties sustained minimal damage

Source: Minnesota Commissioner of Statistics, *Reports*, 1873–77

County had "destroyed fully one-half of all the crops in this county. . . . We are afraid that all will be destroyed before the little pests will leave."[12]

The newly hatched locusts sprouted wings by mid-July and took to the air, leaving the state. New swarms from the West replaced them, and the ravages resumed. Earlier damage had been confined largely to the southwestern part of the state where the eggs had hatched. Now the pests and the destruction spread north and east. Settlers as far north as Moorhead and as far east as Mankato sighted the swarms. Reports were disheartening. By one account, six counties had only an eighth or a tenth of a crop remaining and "In many townships scarcely any [crop] is left, and vegetables are about all destroyed." The *St. Paul Daily Pioneer* reported, "nearly all the farmers in that section [from the Blue Earth River westward] are ruined financially." And that same settler in Martin County who had written so enthusiastically about the wonderful prospects of a crop had to say, "All of those beautiful fields of grain, corn, and potatoes are laid waste, actually eaten up by the grasshoppers."[13]

In the midst of the summer depredations, information about the extent of damage was sometimes sketchy or incorrect. The difficulty of travel and the distance between settlements often left small pockets of settlers isolated from incoming news and misrepresented in outgoing reports. A Nobles County farmer complained about newspaper stories that said his part of the county had not suffered. "I deem it my duty to acquaint you with what I know & *experience* concerning [losses]. My own & several of my neighbors crops are entirely destroyed & were also destroyed last year." Another farmer, who thought the damage in his area had been underestimated, wrote that he had nothing left "except a few peas and 1/10 acre of potatoes which have been eaten down once to the ground and the grasshoppers ate at them again." To emphasize the severity of his troubles, he claimed that the pests "can be found in our houses on our furniture in our clothing and even on our tables at our meals."[14]

The state commissioner of statistics in his annual report estimated the losses of 1874: twenty-eight counties, a considerably larger area than the previous year, sustained serious damages. Eleven percent of the state's total wheat crop was lost, and 16 percent of the oats. Over half the cultivated acreage in the twenty-eight counties was damaged, including 38 percent of the wheat crop and half of the oats. No one computed the losses more carefully than the farmers whose accounts were less precise but as true. The grasshoppers "ate all the grain," according to one farmer. "You couldn't see that there had ever been a cornfield there," said another. A third remembered simply: "No crops were left."[15]

Some farmers faced the partial or total loss of their crops for two successive years; many realized that the yield of 1875 was also threatened, since the grasshoppers again left eggs in the ground. A few, like this man in Murray County, remained optimistic: "We are now happy in being able to report that the grasshoppers are leaving us. . . . No eggs that we know of have yet been laid and we hope for prosperity next summer." But most farmers waited nervously.[16]

In the spring of 1875 the eggs hatched. Many young locusts were killed off by an extended wet and cold snap in the northern parts of the state, and a natural parasite did extensive damage to the eggs in Becker County. In July, when the young developed their wings, they began to migrate out of the state. Unfavorable winds kept most of them from leaving and also shut out new swarms. Damage in 1875 was considerably less than had been feared. The number of counties affected — nineteen — was still large, but the ravages proved less catastrophic than in preceding years. Acreage affected was one-third less than in 1874; average wheat yields returned to 1873 levels, and the crop loss amounted to only a modest 7 percent.[17]

What some hoped would be the end of the plague turned out to be merely the lull before the major storm. A May 1876 report noted that grasshoppers "were spreading themselves over a much greater area than heretofore, and are doing immense damage to the crops." A Lyon County man reported: "The grasshoppers are making a clean sweep of the grain & shrubbery of all kinds, and are not leaving a living thing on improved lands." With a touch of irony, one farmer calculated the number of grasshoppers on his land, estimating at least 150 eggs to each square inch. "At this rate there will be 940,896,000 eggs to the acre, or the nice little pile of 6,586,272,000 on seven acres of my farm." He figured he had enough to supply the whole state if anyone wished to take a few off his hands. Another farmer, with a similarly sardonic sense of humor, wrote: "My early education was somewhat neglected, so I will not attempt to compute the number of hoppers that will be raised to the acre, but will say, from present prospects, they will be 'right smart,' they will be 'powerful' hungry, and will do a heap of damage."[18]

Unfortunately humor did not lessen the seriousness of the 1876

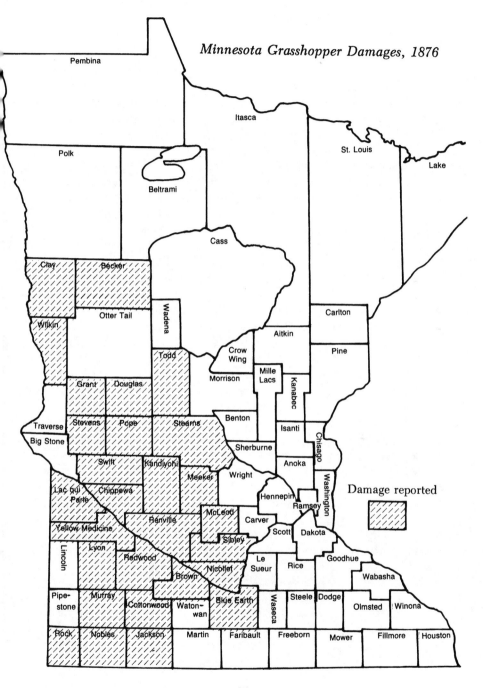

Minnesota Grasshopper Damages, 1876

infestation. Losses were enormous. Twenty-nine counties lost at least part of their crops. The average wheat yield in the state fell to under ten bushels per acre — down from seventeen in 1875. The state lost 16 percent of its wheat crop, 18 percent of its oats, and 15 percent of its corn. Even the least sympathetic could no longer pass the plagues off as a minor difficulty in a distant part of the state.[19]

The 1876 pests left a new crop of eggs. A Norwegian woman wrote to her parents early in 1877 that the grasshoppers "laid an untold number of eggs [and] prospects are very dark for next year. If all the eggs should hatch, there would not be a blade of grass left. . . ." And indeed prospects looked bad. One entomologist predicted that enough eggs would hatch "to lay waste the earth and render it as bare of vegetation as if it is in midwinter." These predictions proved nearly accurate. In mid-May one farmer reported the number of grasshoppers on his farm in the "billion millions." Hatching continued through May and into June and grasshoppers appeared in forty-two counties.[20]

In the middle of the summer the young insects developed their wings on schedule and took to the air. During the previous four years this signaled the beginning of the laying season. For reasons unclear even to entomologists, the young did not move on to adjoining counties to lay their eggs in 1877. Instead they stayed in the air, alighting only occasionally. They were visible overhead for most of the summer, but fewer and fewer came down. After early July the grasshoppers were considered "perfectly harmless," and none laid eggs or even prepared to lay.[21]

The surviving settlers remembered the leaving of the plague as well as they remembered its coming. "Then all of a sudden one fine day . . . a person could see little dark whirlwinds here and there which after a while turned into dark clouds, and lo and behold, it was the grasshoppers leaving in the same manner as they had come several years before. The air grew so thick that the sun could not be seen and the grasshoppers were gone." Another recalled, "one day they all left. I don't know as I have seen a grasshopper here since."[22]

No one really knew why the grasshoppers left. The entomologists could not adequately explain it. Only the religious had an answer. Governor John S. Pillsbury had declared a day of prayer for April 26, 1877, calling on citizens to plead for deliverance from this plague. A few days after the prayer day, one settler remembered, "the grasshoppers rose in a body clouding the sunshine and left for parts un-

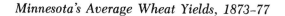

Minnesota's Average Wheat Yields, 1873–77

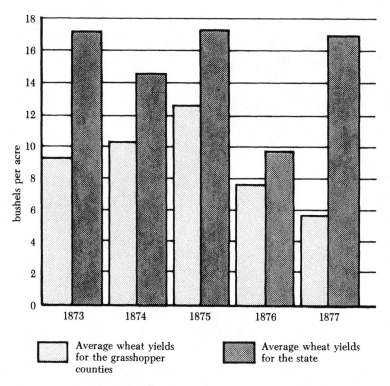

The total bushels of wheat produced in Minnesota are as follows:
1872 – 22,059,375   1874 – 23,938,172   1876 – 17,964,632
1873 – 26,402,485   1875 – 30,079,300   1877 – 30,693,969
Source: Minnesota Commissioner of Statistics, *Reports*, 1872–77

known never to return and I certainly believe in answers coming to prayer."[23]

The American Tract Society drew the same conclusion; in 1878 it published a pamphlet explaining the mysterious disappearance of the insects. Within twelve hours after the prayer day, it reported, "A very remarkable change in the weather occurred." An April snowstorm with hard frost set in and lasted for two days. The pamphlet did not claim that all the grasshoppers died immediately or even that they all suddenly arose in a body and disappeared, but it did contend that after the prayers and the storm the pests behaved "as grass-

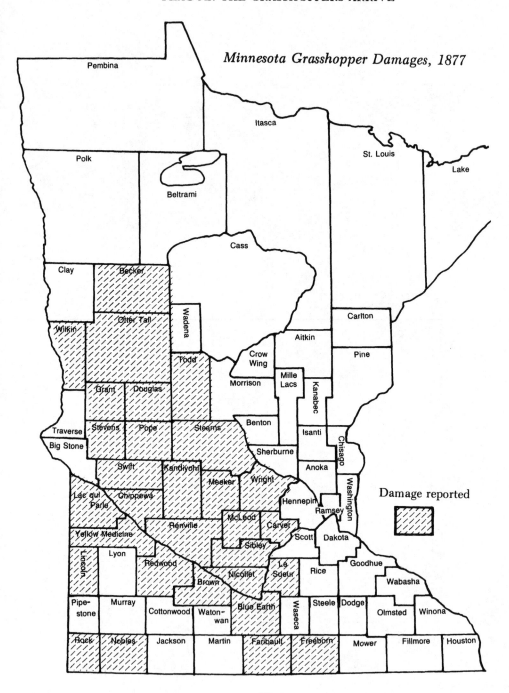

Minnesota Grasshopper Damages, 1877

hoppers are not known to have done before." The society attributed this deliverance from the scourge to the "Christians' faith" and the "Christians' God."[24]

Whether it was the efficacy of prayer, the end of a cycle, or adverse weather conditions, the pests left in 1877, having again done extensive damage. Farmers lost almost five million bushels of wheat, almost two million bushels of oats, and two million bushels of corn. Grain crops constituted almost 94 percent of Minnesota's cultivated acreage; 15 percent of that was ruined. Some farmers in the state had indeed harvested wonderful yields and full crops; others suffered badly again. But they realized that the scourge had ended. They did not face loss to grasshoppers in 1878. Perhaps finally they could reap the promise of this land that was Minnesota.

One faithful diarist left pithy, year-end comments that aptly describe the events and the character of each year (apparently having been spared in 1873).

> December 31, 1874: "The year closed with three days of very cold weather. No great events have occurred to make the last year noted. Political dissentions [sic] in the south, the success of the Democrats at the elections, temperance revivals, the Beecher-Tilton scandal, 'hard times' and grasshopper raids in the northwestern states, about makes up the sum of good and evil."
> December 31, 1875: "It has been a year in which, from first to last, there have been widespread complaints of hard times."
> December 31, 1876: "The grasshoppers have destroyed a large amount of crops and the prospect is discouraging for the coming year."
> December 31, 1877: "In reviewing the events of the closing twelve months it is notable that Minnesota emerged clothed in the golden glory of such a harvest as was never before seen. It was the year when the grasshoppers took their final flight, and 35,000,000. bushels of the finest wheat that grew were garnered in our granaries. A memorable year, if for only these two events alone, and for the consequent impulse they gave to the prosperity of the State, to the revival of all kinds of business, and to the tide of immigration which, since harvest, has been pouring into our frontier counties on a scale much larger than has been known for years."[25]

The plague was over.

3

The Farmers React

Hampered by inexperience and by the sheer numbers of grasshoppers, the settlers did not know what to do when the insects first arrived. A few people stood by helplessly. One woman simply sank to her knees and wailed: "The locusts! God help us!" Others acted quickly to do what they could. "For a moment Rosie stood confused and aghast. Then her natural self-reliance returned," wrote one settler about his mother. "'Well, let's go out and cut what we can,' she said. She grabbed her bonnet from a nail on the wall, shook the grasshoppers out of it, and in a minute was ready." Like many a historical character, the fictional Per Hansa grabbed his gun and fired into the swarms. Others clanged pans and tin cans; they waved their arms and yelled; they rang bells. Many a woman hoped to save her garden by covering it with blankets or rags, only to see the garden, the blankets, and the rags chewed up. Others burned straw or walked through the fields swinging ropes or shaking the plants to keep the insects from alighting.[1]

From 1873 through 1875, farmers made individual, isolated attempts to destroy the pests. They lighted smudge pots to keep them in flight; they deliberately set prairie fires to kill the fledglings. Some settlers captured grasshoppers in buckets or by hand or by shovel. During 1876 and 1877 this last method was used on a larger scale. Amateur inventors worked up various methods for grasshopper-killing machines called "hopperdozers." The most practical, cheapest to build, and easiest to operate barely merited the compliment of being called a machine. It required only a piece of sheet metal smeared with coal tar (or molasses, which was less effective, but cheaper and more readily available). Two people, or one person with a horse, could drag this device through a field. The forward motion forced the grasshoppers into the pan where they got caught in the tar. At the end of each row the pan would be emptied into a fire. Hopperdozer dragging could go on for days. Mothers and fathers, sons and daughters, adults and children did their part. Neighbors and communities worked together. In Kandiyohi County alone — apparently the only place where a count was made — the people made or bought over six hundred hopperdozers.[2]

None of these efforts helped much in lessening the damages. The pests did not scare easily, smoke did not deter them, attempts to catch them were futile. As one farmer reported, "Every device that the ingenuity of man could devise was resorted to [to] kill them off, and they still increased." The hopperdozer reportedly "thinned out" the grasshopper population in some places; elsewhere it was useless. The grasshoppers did their damage "faster than you can kill them with any device yet invented."[3]

Any right-thinking farmer — at least one who refused to give up — did what he could to save his crops. In that, the settlers of southwestern Minnesota were not unusual. They fought and continued fighting the pests even in the face of repeated failure. Why? Certainly the farmers were fighting the insects to get rid of them. But the greater value of their efforts may have been psychological, although they could not have identified it as such. By combating the pests they were doing *something*, thereby warding off the feelings of helplessness occasioned by a natural disaster that no one understood and against which there could be no effective protection. They fought, too, so that they could believe they controlled their own future. If they just worked hard enough they would succeed — even where success was impossible. Insofar as they honored the American work ethic, they believed that success followed hard work. If the work ethic did not explain how work resulted in failure, then how could these people explain it to the world, each other, themselves?

A peculiar optimism characterized the victims — an optimism based on denying the threat and minimizing the danger. While farmers of southwestern Minnesota had little experience with Rocky Mountain locusts, they nonetheless understood uncertainty and losses. Even the most unrealistic knew that they were involved in a risky business. Natural disasters of a dozen varieties always threatened. When bad weather and disease held off, farmers still had to contend with seemingly capricious prices. Yet they tried to ignore the menace that the grasshoppers posed.

At the end of the first season in 1873 the settlers wanted to believe that the pests had done all the damage they would and and that the worst was over. "Our hopes soon rose," one settler recalled, "and our courage was braced as we cheered ourselves with the thought that this was but for one year." Another remembered, "Our doom was upon us. How serious it was we could not realize at the time." The farmers demonstrated their optimism (or hope) by regularly issuing premature declarations of deliverance. Finding grasshopper eggs in their fields, they confidently told each other that the eggs could not possibly survive a Minnesota winter, or a reported predatory insect, or a wet spring, or any number of other potential saviors. When the eggs hatched and the young set to eating, settlers still believed that not much harm would be done. "The majority of people here think [the grasshoppers] will not damage us to any extent," wrote a Watonwan County man. A Jackson County optimist echoed this sentiment. "The prospects for an abundant harvest have never been better," he wrote, although the eggs had already hatched "in great numbers" in his area and whole fields had been destroyed. Another farmer whose ground was sown with eggs predicted a bright future nonetheless. "If no calamity befalls this region a bountiful harvest will be reapt [sic] and a Season of perpetual prosperity inaugurated."[4]

Ole Rølvaag caught this spirit in *Giants in the Earth.* "And all the while the folk tried to comfort one another. . . . It will be better by-and-by, you know! . . . I'll bet my last dollar, some one else would venture, that next year everything will be all right! . . . And when it turned out to be just as bad the following year, the same person would be even more confident. Now, see — we've had this thing with us two years already — this is the end. . . . And even when the third summer came, and there was no let up in the awful visitation, some bright head would remember the indisputable fact that *all good things are three.* So there! — Now let's thank the Lord that we're through with it at last!" And inexorably, the plague returned again and again. The same spirit prevailed in other novels. In *A Lantern in Her Hand,* Will Deal believed fiercely in the future. "The land hasn't turned against us. . . . Some day this is going to be the richest state in the union . . . the most productive," he argued, "I'll bet anything next year. . . ," but he never finished the sentence.[5]

When an attack ended, the settlers set about assessing the damages. Some saved part of their crop, largely through the capriciousness of the grasshoppers, and did not face immediate hardship. Even the worst-hit counties showed at least small harvests each year. These few bushels kept families fed for a time. A handful of farmers even salvaged enough grain to ship some to market. For them, the grasshoppers represented an unfortunate setback, but no desolation. Some two hundred people in Martin County's English colony faced no serious recovery problems. The resident "remittance men," as they were called, received regular allowances from their wealthy English families. Anyone who did not depend entirely upon his crops could make do, even start over.

Those who did lose crops or did not benefit from family connections or other outside income faced a rough time. As the *St. Paul Daily Pioneer* reported, "Go where you will gloom pervades many an otherwise happy household." Many settlers faced "great destitution & distress," according to one observer. "The prospect is appalling to the poor man with a large family who has exhausted all & sees no return for his labor."[6]

Some settlers simply quit. They hitched their wagon to a new star and moved on. They went east or west, it did not matter so long as there were no grasshoppers. An eastern Minnesota newspaper told of a party of emigrants who passed through with wagons "ornamented on each side with pictures of the pest — accompanied by appropriate and very expressive epithets in condemnation of the same." In another caravan one wagon sported only a drawing of a grasshopper captioned "He Wins."[7]

Among those who left southwestern Minnesota were Laura Ingalls Wilder and her family. In 1876 they moved to northern Iowa where they ran a hotel for the next few years. They lost more than their claim and their dream of being independent. Her infant brother died on the trip.[8]

Grasshopper-damaged counties underwent dramatic slowdowns in population growth during the plague years. A few lost population. Watonwan County, for example, after almost doubling its population from 1870 to 1873, declined 11 percent during the next two years. Martin County experienced an even more startling downturn. Fewer people lived there in 1875 than in 1870 — a nearly unheard-of occurrence in a frontier area. Clearly, thousands of farm families in southwestern Minnesota decided to try their luck elsewhere.[9]

Life in the nineteenth century did not involve for most people a commitment to permanence, tradition, and stability, at least geographically. More often than not, the roots planted in one place were left to wither while new ones were put down in another. Searching, hoping for a better way of life, thousands of Americans tried one spot for a time, abandoned it, and moved on again. Agricultural disaster compounded this tendency. Early studies of rural mobility demonstrated that net population figures disguised enormous movement in and out of rural communities. "Moving Americans" with fever in their blood and an itch in their feet populated the farming frontier. Thus, even more people left southwestern Minnesota than the census figures indicate.[10]

Perhaps, however, what the census figures show is not an unusual loss of population, but a dramatic decrease in the numbers of people who moved in to take the out-migrants' places. In normally prosperous communities newcomers quickly replaced those who left. But in the mid-1870s in southwestern Minnesota, few stopped to make their homes. They took their dreams elsewhere. Homestead entries suggest this loss of new population. The land office in Worthington recorded an average of 946 initial entries annually between 1871 and 1873. Between 1874 and 1877 these figures dropped by almost two-thirds, to an average of only 354 per year. During the three years following the plagues, 1878–80, the average number of entries increased, not to the high levels of the early 1870s, but to almost a hundred more annually than in the mid-1870s. There were fewer in 1875 than in any other year of the decade.[11]

In the face of disaster, some farm families gave up temporarily, staying with friends or relatives, or returning to their former homes for a time. The Carpenters — Mary, George, and their children — were one such family. In June 1873, at about the same time the grasshoppers were moving eastward, the Carpenters moved from Rochester westward to Lyon County — a journey of nearly two hundred miles that took about two weeks. Mary drove the wagon; the children rode some and walked some; George walked most of the way, leading the stock.[12]

In July Mary described her journey and the family's troubles to her Aunt Martha in Connecticut in a letter penciled on wrinkled paper (for which Mary apologized). They had planned to sell their horse when they arrived but could find no buyer. Their best cow got sick on the trip and recovered slowly. Most of their goods, including clothing, furniture, household items, even Mary's ink, remained in storage because they could not raise the thirty dollars they owed on the railroad freight bill. And, finally, the grasshoppers destroyed the gardens, so only a few potatoes were growing.

Mary, six months pregnant, faced the future with some fear and anxiety. "I am trying to trust in God's promises, but we can't expect him to work miracles nowadays." And she worried about herself in this venture. She confessed to being not "romantic enough" to have enjoyed the trip much, nor endowed with sufficient "pioneering spirit" for her new life. "My taste," she wrote, "runs . . . to conveniences, elegancies, comforts and all the paraphernalia of civilized life." She did believe, however, that although the first two years would be hard, "If we struggle through them, then we stand a chance to do pretty well, I think."

A second letter, written to another aunt three months later, made it clear that they could not quite struggle through. Mary and her new baby — ten and a quarter pounds at birth in early October — had already moved in with a neighbor for greater warmth and comfort than the Carpenter's own ten-square-foot shanty provided. She awaited money from the aunt so that she and her family could set off on their return trip to Rochester. "We are anxious to get back to Rochester as soon as possible," she wrote, "but we have no money and cannot go without any. . . ." She added, "If you have not already sent the money, will you please send five or ten dollars . . . as soon as you get this?" The money must have arrived, because the Carpenters returned to Rochester for the winter. In the spring of 1874 they moved back to Lyon County, only to leave again for the winter of 1874–75.[13]

Sometimes only the men left in search of seasonal work. During the winter the pineries of northern Minnesota promised employment, as did Minneapolis and St. Paul from time to time. Farm work in eastern Minnesota offered the best opportunities in spring and, in particular, fall. In the harvest fields near Rochester, Laura Ingalls Wilder's father met many who, like himself, had nothing of their own to harvest so got paid to help others.

Finding work away from home provided financial support but could cause suffering too. "I would like to see you David," a Jackson County woman wrote to her husband, who was working temporarily in Olmsted County. "I am sick and need your love and kind words to help me along, not your written courage. I think we are both striving with all our might to better our condition shall we succeed that is the question. . . ."[14]

Southwestern Minnesota lost settlers during the dark days of the 1870s — those who up and left, permanently or temporarily, as well as those who never arrived, but thousands remained. Some could afford to stay; some could not afford to leave. Debts held some. Others wanted to hold on to their investments of time and energy. Some felt different attachments; as one man explained, "I have lost my all here, & somehow I believe that if I find it again, it will be in the immediate neighborhood where I lost it. . . ." More important, he wrote, "I have a child buried on my claim, & my ties here are stronger & more binding on that account."[15]

One who stayed was Theodore G. Carter — farmer, land agent, and horticulturist in Nicollet County near St. Peter. He left a record of his trials. Over four years he watched his farm, business, and financial security disintegrate. In 1874 he lost most of his nursery stock, including over four thousand grapevines — his pride and joy. He knew the fate of his 1875 crop as early as June: "Crops either gone or fast going." Before the season ended he lost his fifteen acres of wheat, five hundred cabbages, all his cucumbers, beans, onions, carrots, parsnips, and beets. He saved part of his oats, corn, potatoes, melons, and apple trees, plus one-fifth of his tomatoes. He estimated that he could have made over three hundred dollars on strawberries and raspberries alone. Instead, he earned about twenty-two dollars. In 1876 and 1877 he saw virtual re-enactments of the troubles of the preceding two years.[16]

His horticulture business also suffered. What the grasshoppers left, Carter could not sell. Plagued by insufficient funds, most farmers could not afford "luxuries" such as fruit trees and nursery stock, and the market for them dried up completely. Carter's real-estate business diminished, too. By the end of 1874 sales "almost entirely ceased," with little prospect of improvement. Two years later the market remained the same: "Real estate is down no sale at any price hardly."[17]

With his crops and business failing, Carter faced a severe financial situation. He had been in the horticulture business for only three years when the first wave of grasshoppers swept through. Counting on the sure success of his crops, he borrowed five thousand dollars from the Aetna Life Insurance Company. But in late December 1874 he had to request an extension: "Up to the present time I have always met my payments large & small punctually, and I flatter myself my reputation for promptness is A.1. at the Banks and with the business men generally." Nonetheless, he could not pay. Unyielding, the company notified Carter that it would foreclose on his land. He offered the insurance company a deal: he would send them a quit-claim on the land and save them the time and cost of attorneys' fees in exchange for a grace period of thirteen months to redeem the land; the details of foreclosing would take at least that long. Although Aetna agreed, Carter still faced money problems. He could not pay other debts, including one for seventy-five dollars owed to a friend. He made deals, tried to strike bargains, offered to pay interest on the interest — anything to get through the hard years.[18]

In a further effort to meet his obligations, Carter called in loans that he had extended in better days. To one debtor he wrote, "As I am extremely hard up for money, and as I have waited a year and over more than the two weeks you asked me to wait, I am compelled to ask you for the amount due me $12.50 and interest." With a hardness forged by desperation, he demanded that the money be sent "before January 1st *without fail.*" Six months later he wrote to another in his debt, "money due and nothing to pay with, and need the amount of my bill badly. I have had to borrow money and now the interest is due and I cannot meet that. Do send me $50. without fail or delay." A year later Carter still waited for repayments that did not come. He could not collect and he could not pay.[19]

The combination of financial troubles and the harsh winter of 1875 convinced Carter that he should move: "For the first time in about 19 years I feel like emigrating to a land where it never freezes." The more he thought about it, the better he liked the idea. "The wear and tear of this debt business is too much for me." In May he decided that if the grasshoppers cleaned him out, "I cannot help it. I am about ready to emigrate any way." He set his sights on Florida, and his dream of moving gradually took shape. He wrote to his cousin, "My worst trouble just now is to get out of Min. with money enough to take us to Florida." He never did get sufficient funds together. It took everything he had just to hold on. He used up his life savings, sold his prize Jersey bull and most of his other livestock, let his hired man go, and gave up his cherished newspapers. "If the grasshoppers keep on as they have commenced," he wrote when his subscription to a New York paper ran out, "economy will be a necessity and papers a luxury."[20]

Carter's neighbors had it no better. In 1874 he reported, "People are not paying their debts." Two years later the problem of repayments was forgotten in the struggle simply to stay afloat: "Even the necessary funds to pay rent, fuel &c. bears hard on our numbers here. With the most of us it is a question of *necessaries* of life. . . ." Later he voiced his fear that the current visitation of the pests "will bankrupt thousands who had already all they could stand up under." And it did bankrupt Carter, who finally moved, not to Florida, but to St. Peter.[21]

Not until late 1877 did he see any brightening of his plight. "We hope now that the 'great army' has left for a season," he wrote, "and under this belief there is prospect of business, real estate begins to look up & there are some sales." The threat of renewed raids lifted and "people began to regain confidence." Carter and his neighbors were not yet out of the woods, but with a good harvest in 1878 they could start again. "Everything is looking brighter now and I think next year will be the most prosperous of any that have been experienced in Minnesota." Carter drew a lesson from these hard times: "This life is mixed up of joy and sorrow, and I think on the whole sorrow predominated, perhaps it is best it should [,] so that we shall be weaned from an attachment to earth and its vanities."[22]

Like Carter, most farmers tried a variety of ways to help themselves. When they faced severe shortages they tried to mortgage their property — a forbidding prospect. The nationwide depression of the 1870s had tightened the money supply. Furthermore, so long as the pests threatened, land proved to be poor security for loans. As a Rock County farmer complained, "I have tried to borrow money but cannot do it." Carter had mentioned the problem: "I have been to every man that had any money, but money is scarce here, and people will not go out of their own Co[unty] to loan and to tell you the truth intelligent men do not like to loan on that . . . property." In Martin County, for example, mortgages were hard to secure. In 1872, 246 mortgages were recorded, a total unequaled in any other year of the decade; less than half the 1872 number were filed in 1874.[23]

When real estate could not be mortgaged, farmers turned to personal property. In one Chippewa County township, the number of chattel mortgages increased dramatically in the mid-1870s. In 1873 only thirty were recorded; in 1874, more than two and a half times as many — seventy-six. The number continued high until 1878, when it declined to fifty-three. The rate of satisfaction of the chattel mortgages also reflected the hard times. In 1872 nearly half were satisfied and in 1877 only a quarter were.[24]

Instead of mortgaging, some sold their horses or other livestock. They postponed land improvements. When crops failed they gathered wild berries and went fishing for food. One woman told about a sudden increase in the number of buffalo fish in local rivers — "more than anyone had ever seen" — that helped many families through the hard years. Some farmers planted corn or peas or beans or any crops that they hoped were not so vulnerable as wheat. In Jackson County, for example, farmers sowed about eight thousand acres in wheat in 1873 — nearly 64 percent of their property — and only just over one thousand acres, or 8 percent, in corn. By 1877 the planting patterns had completely reversed: almost five thousand acres in corn — 47 percent — and sixteen hundred acres in wheat — 16 percent. Some optimistic observers asserted that the silver lining of the plague cloud was that it forced farmers to diversify and dethroned wheat as king. This was not quite true. Jackson County, like other areas, reverted almost immediately to wheat when the hard times passed. In 1878 wheat shot back up to nearly 63 percent of the acreage and corn dropped to about 12 percent. [25]

Lacking sufficient money and seed, many farmers simply planted less. In Jackson County the total acreage in the three major crops — wheat, oats, and corn — declined by almost 60 percent between 1875 and 1877 from over twenty thousand to under eight thousand. The acreage planted in these three crops in Martin County declined by almost half — from over twenty-six thousand acres in 1873 to under fourteen thousand in 1877 — and did not recover until the end of the plague in 1878, when farmers planted twenty thousand acres. [26]

Some people, finding human remedies futile, turned to spiritual assistance. They prayed. If a god had sent this plague, as in the Bible, only that god could lift it. So year after year they begged for deliverance; they pleaded for forgiveness of their sins; they made promises in exchange for the cup being passed from them. Catholics near Cold Spring pledged themselves to build a chapel if the scourge would be lifted. [27]

Others tried humor — usually sardonic — to ease the emotional aspect of the plague. For months a Martin County store advertised, "EVERYTHING SOLD AT GRASSHOPPER PRICES!!" One farmer, advised to smoke the insects out, replied, "I tried it and the little pests came down to warm their legs by my fire." And then there was the dialogue between teacher and student that, reportedly, always raised shouts of laughter:

39

Teacher: Where does all our grain go?
Student: Into the hopper.
Teacher: What hopper?
Student: Grasshopper![28]

These methods did not help much, except perhaps to lighten the settlers' spirits. Most people, however, needed money or relief of some kind and could not get it themselves. Some, like Mary Carpenter, appealed to friends and relatives outside of the grasshopper country. To her Aunt Martha in Connecticut, Mary wrote, "if you happen to have any old things that you don't think worth sending they would do us lots of good." She received help from several relatives. They sent her money, clothing, household goods, even "a nice lot of stationery, paper and a package of stamped envelopes" so Mary could keep on writing.[29]

Other people called on distant acquaintances. One Renville County man wrote to a St. Paul doctor who had treated a family member some six years earlier. The letter began, "I don't know if you remember me. . . ." and went on to appeal to the doctor's sympathy and generosity.[30]

A few settlers took the responsibility upon themselves to launch a formal appeal through selected national publications and organizations. A Worthington woman sent to *The Little Corporal* — a national children's magazine — an article describing the plight of the children of southwestern Minnesota. She called on youngsters to form aid societies to help their suffering brothers and sisters on the frontier. A Steele County minister wrote to the New York *Christian Advocate*, "endeavoring to give the friends in the East an intelligent idea of how numerous the grasshoppers really were," and thereby encouraging assistance.[31]

Others turned to the state government. Throughout the plague years hundreds of settlers besieged officials with requests for help. Some simply described their personal conditions. A Murray County woman begged for goods, clothing, and bedding. She and her father had but two quilts and two sheets with neither beds nor a floor to protect them from the cold. They found it "most impossible to keep warm." A Norwegian farmer told a familiar story. "Wee are now used cleand out we never give up till now we have nothin to fell back on we are 8 in famely we have weark hard two seve our Bread but all two no use we are out meens and money provisions and clothing we have no boots nor shose and no meanes two get Dem namore at present."[32]

Sometimes individuals banded together to ask for help. They drew up petitions, witnessed by a justice of the peace or county or township official to give them added weight and validity. A group of Lyon County citizens, in a plea certified by their postmaster and their county commissioner, attested to their "suffering Condition" and asked the state to "take Some Measure to Render us Assistance as soon as Possible." The victims asked for whatever help could be given, or they asked specifically for seed, food, fuel, clothing, yarn to knit stockings, or a job—no matter how "humble." Most of them did not mention why others ought to help. They did not offer justifications; they only asked or begged for mercy and generosity.[33]

But some settlers, in their requests to the state government, threatened rather than begged. Using the only leverage available to them, they said they would leave the state if help were not forthcoming. State officials heard the same message repeatedly: "We must leave and that soon if we cannot get help"; "Unless those high in authority can do something for us soon we must abandon our homes"; "unless something be done outside of us, we will be compelled to abandon our homes in the far west"; or, finally, "The fact seems to be that there are numerous farmers in our county, whom bleak-eyed starvation looks right square in the face . . . if no help is extended to them they must and will leave."[34]

Nineteenth-century attitudes that held the needy responsible for their condition played a role in the outlook and response of some of the victims. Some who shared the prevailing ideas about the poor preferred to suffer rather than take help. A Jackson County woman wrote to her husband, who was looking for work in eastern Minnesota. "David if possible do not beg. I should be so ashamed to face people after begging my way to them. . . ." Even though they could not raise money to reunite the family or to buy shoes for their children and even though their farmhouse was so cold that this woman feared death from freezing, she asked her husband to "try to borrow money . . . before you solicit aid from Strangers. . . ." Better to suffer than to lose their self-respect by begging.[35]

Reportedly others, too, refused assistance. "There are many families who are heroically enduring their loss," a Worthington man observed. They were "taking every pains to conceal their real condition they will not consent to receive any assistance till they approach the verge of starvation." These noble souls, he continued, would rather eat boiled grass and weeds "than disgrace themselves, and the community in which they live, by applying for relief, and appearing before the world as mendicants." Another reported that "hundreds are ashamed to beg or acknowledge their destitution, hundreds are preferring to sell their stock and [leave] for more [bountiful] places to begin at the bottom once more." Still another commented that people suffered because of their "repugnance to the reception of charity. . . ."[36]

When victims joined together to ask for assistance, they often took a more aggressive position than did individuals alone. Constituting themselves as ad hoc relief committees, groups drew up formal appeals to "The Charitable of our State," or "The People of the United States," or newspapers, or any group of outsiders who would pay attention. They offered practical grounds for their requests: they had already endured losses and more seemed inevitable. They pleaded their case melodramatically: "What shall we do when winter rages wrathfully over these bleak prairies and our children cry for bread?" They prayed for Christian duty: "Prove not yourselves worthy of God's mercies by offering . . . a stone." They claimed patriotic duty: "Forget not how danger jointly shared [in the Civil War] made us brethren. . . ."[37]

The settlers' most strongly emphasized arguments, however, demonstrated how dearly they held the notions that charity was ill advised and demoralizing, that assistance rewarded the unworthy, and that poverty resulted from personal failure. The appeals, rather than repudiating these ideas, gave them credence by honoring them. The pleas overtly rejected the application of these attitudes to the stricken settlers by arguing that the victims had an abundance of good American virtues.

The appeals, for example, paid particular attention to the hard-working nature of the settlers. They could not be accused of laziness nor suspected of trying to take unfair advantage of generosity. As one circular stated, no "lack of industry" caused the settlers' need. Indeed, "All that industry can do in such circumstances our people will do to help themselves." If people could help themselves further or could refrain from asking for aid, they would do so, "but what shall we do when labor will not buy us bread and economy becomes useless because there is nothing to economize?" Another called attention to the "untiring energy and undaunted courage" of the settlers. Yet another stated specifically that the destitute were a "temperate, intelligent, industrious, moral class of people" who were trying to build a future for themselves and for their children.[38]

Another appeal openly claimed the right of victims to aid. As "greatly distressed people" suffering from a disaster "beyond human power to withstand, or beat back," the citizens "feel that we have the right to petition and pray for aid from those other states of this Country who have been more fortunate than ourselves." If another state were invaded by a "public foe or enemy," the plea argued, Minnesotans would be called on to render aid, perhaps even be asked for the "laying down of our lives and the spilling of our blood. . . ." It continued, "we as a part of the people of the United States, under the protection of the whole . . . feel . . . that we have the right and that it is our duty to claim that protection naturally due us." They asked not for the blood of their countrymen but for food for their families.[39]

These settlers did not talk about charity and benevolence; they talked about rights and obligations. They refused to see themselves as mendicants. They were not ready to abandon the ideology that attributed poverty to individual and moral weaknesses. They wanted only to be excluded from that category themselves. They knew at first hand that poverty often bore little relationship to human conduct, that success did not come easily, and that it resulted only in part from hard work. They knew that luck, chance, politics, money, and power all played important roles. Yet these settlers did not change their nineteenth-century ideas about poverty and the poor. They did not offer a new and radical critique of the social system that blamed the poor, nor did they seriously question a governmental system that allowed people to suffer. They just wanted help. They asked for it in a way that would leave them free of blame, that adhered to common values about the poor, and that might get them some aid. Many settlers were to be disappointed when their requests yielded so little, with so many strings.

4

Counties Face the Challenge

How the settlers' needs should be met, and by whom, persisted as unresolved questions throughout the plague years. Since no one suspected that the devastation would be so severe or for so long, the question of responsibility was never formally addressed. Most observers saw the disaster as temporary and, therefore, like any other agricultural calamity. The poor made do and the better off made do better. But this was unlike any other agricultural problem — it affected too many people for too long a time.

Communities in the early 1870s had not set policy for handling disaster relief. State governments had not decided beforehand where local responsibility ended and state responsibility began — or even whether the state had an obligation to offer assistance. Without conscious and thoughtful consideration of this situation, individuals and groups responded to appeals on the basis of preconceived notions. Each effort by a group followed the exigencies of time and circumstances, and the programs were piecemeal, ad hoc, and sometimes spontaneous. This disaster did not force individuals or groups to think differently, so the relief efforts reflected the values and dispositions of the time.

When the needy called for help, they discovered that neither public nor private charities could meet the demand. State statutes paid no particular attention to poverty occasioned by natural affliction. The Act for the Relief of the Poor, passed in 1849 by the Minnesota territorial legislature, defined those eligible for public aid as "Every poor person who is unable to earn a livelihood in consequence of bodily infirmity, idiocy, lunacy or other cause." It stipulated that individuals should, if at all possible, take care of themselves. If they were unable to, they should turn to relatives. If relatives could not or would not, under threat of prosecution, provide adequate help,

44

the responsibility fell to county authorities. This law, and earlier versions of it in the Old Northwest, New England, and England on which it was based, assumed that the number of needy at any one time would be small. Only those unfit to make a living could legitimately qualify for public relief. These would be few, and the meager budgets of county governments could bear the financial burden.[1]

In the nineteenth century few people imagined a situation in which those who worked hard still found themselves unable to manage. That such cases occurred with some frequency, particularly among urban laborers subject to the dislocations of economic cycles, did not force a change in the dominant ideology that held individuals responsible for their own poverty. Thus the law did not cover a situation of widespread or prolonged need requiring public assistance.

Private charities shared the assumption that only a few would be legitimately needy at any one time. They were prepared, therefore, to handle a few cases, but not thousands, at once. Moreover, most private charities that existed in Minnesota in the 1870s were urban institutions. A variety of permanent private organizations assisted the needy in Minneapolis and St. Paul. Focused on urban problems and patterned on the Associations for Improving the Condition of the Poor or the Associated Charities of New York, Chicago, and Boston, the Twin Cities organizations were designed to deal in a limited way with specific local problems. The Mary Magdalen Society, for example, cared for "fallen women"; the Young Men's Christian Association helped farm boys adjust to city life; the Citizens' Relief Association aided a few people who did not qualify for county relief. These groups were not designed to help thousands of needy farmers. Indeed, such charitable organizations did not exist in rural areas. Nationwide, the American Red Cross had not yet been founded and the Salvation Army operated only in England.[2]

The vague wording of the Minnesota poor law — holding county governments solely responsible for those unable to earn a livelihood due to any "other cause" — would seem to have qualified needy farm families for assistance and to have made the county commissioners the primary agents for care. Local officials in southwestern Minnesota knew at first hand the effects of the plagues: the unlucky ones through personal experience and the more fortunate through observation of friends and neighbors. Moved by genuine sympathy and concern, some commissioners may have wanted to help. In their capacity as elected officials and besieged by pleas for assistance, some may have believed they bore a responsibility to help. But in late 1873 and early 1874 most county boards chose not to act. Certainly counties could not afford the expense, and perhaps commissioners did not know what they could or should do. They realized they were charged with caring for the "poor," but these farmers did not fit that category precisely.

In Martin County, a representative but not entirely typical area, the subject never appears as business in the minutes of commissioners' meetings. Only in January 1874 did the officials turn their attention to plague victims when the newly elected state representative asked the board to investigate the need for seed grain. The board formed a committee and reported its findings. The plague issue did not emerge again in either 1874 or 1875.[3]

The absence of statutory mandate, of established private organizations in rural areas, and of urban organizations that held themselves to rural obligations, meant that no one had a clearly defined responsibility to help the needy farmers. Therefore, a few people at the local and county levels took the initiative. At one extreme, a group of Lyon County citizens denied that public response was necessary. In early 1874 a "citizens" meeting convened in Lyon County to "ascertain the truth" about the effects of the plagues. The participants came armed, they said, with the "truth." They bitterly accused the newspapers of exaggerating the settlers' needs and of presenting an overly bleak picture of conditions. They maintained that no one suffered from lack of food, clothing, or shelter. Yes, they knew that a family here or an individual there faced hardship, but neighbors helped out when it was necessary.

At the meeting a leading citizen announced that in wide travels throughout the county he had not observed a single case of destitution. He had heard rumors of two families in a remote area who needed help, the first officially reported in the entire county. To him and to his listeners these exceptions proved the rule. Their willingness to acknowledge these cases, they said, showed that the participants at the meeting had no desire to hide or disguise the need where it existed. According to them, poverty simply did not exist in the county.

Citizens at the meeting did, however, know about attempts to defraud the charitable and get what was not needed. Individuals

46

who could adequately support themselves were, reportedly, crying for public charity. In one particularly "disgusting" case, a farmer who was "abundantly able to take care of himself" — according to his neighbors — had appealed outside of the county for assistance. Out of purely base and selfish interests, they said, this man had injured the "fair name" of the county.[4]

The participants formed a committee to investigate legitimate cases of destitution. After inquiring whether the needy could satisfy their own wants by the "sale of property or otherwise," the committee could take count and thereby stifle unfounded and damaging tales of widespread poverty. They adopted a resolution condemning newspapers that falsely reported need in Lyon County, and they censured citizens who fraudulently appealed for outside assistance. Before the meeting adjourned, the participants passed another resolution effectively canceling the investigation. They concluded: "Diligent and careful inquiry has been made in all sections to discover any cases of extreme poverty, destitution that may exist" and none had been found. Therefore, all reports of need in Lyon County were "utterly false." Furthermore, if any cases came to light, the county could take care of its own.

These participants may have stated conditions accurately, but neither the statistical reports of damages nor other accounts from and about Lyon County substantiated the charges about exaggeration. The meeting did, however, give voice to a serious tension that existed within many of the stricken counties. The grasshoppers did not damage all crops equally in all places. Individuals or whole townships could lose entire fields while neighbors escaped such misfortune. This did not simply indicate that only some farmers asked for help, but could also set up serious differences of interest within a county. Farm people who lost crops and faced hardships benefited from widespread publicity about the damages, yet news about destitution, even about the plagues themselves, could harm the county as a whole. Virtually every frontier county saw its long-range success and prosperity as dependent upon growth, which required a constant stream of new settlers. The best encouragement for new settlement was the demonstrated productivity and promise of a particular corner of the frontier. Lyon County boosters, for example, had to persuade prospective settlers that their area offered more than Worth County, Iowa, or Minnehaha County, Dakota Territory, or any one of hundreds of other possible stopping places. News of grasshopper

47

plagues and the resulting destitution could effectively discourage settlers.

In other counties private groups responded not by rejecting the appeals but by forming ad hoc relief committees. Each set its own agenda, timetable, and tactics. In Jackson County the citizens formed two groups — one to investigate the local need and the other to explore sources of funding outside of the county. A Nobles County central committee appointed township groups to investigate and to provide "such aid as may be found necessary." Easier said, of course, than done. The Nobles committee did not stipulate where to obtain such aid. None of the groups had funds, so each had to go searching. Some counties issued appeals to the residents of the state and the generous of the nation. Others appointed solicitors to raise contributions outside Minnesota. Virtually all the committees turned to the state government for help.[5]

Throughout the fall and winter of 1873-74 these groups carried the major responsibility for care of the needy. By late May 1874 most people realized that the grasshopper depredations would not only recur but would increase. Where the grasshoppers damaged crops for the first time, farmers would eventually require help to get through the winter. Where the insects were making a second sweep in two years, however, the settlers faced urgent needs. Furthermore, some families that had survived a first bad year without help could not survive a second.

As soon as the fate of the 1874 crops became obvious, the private county committees again set to work. First they agreed to organize county conventions where town supervisors would report on conditions in their areas. Delegates could then take this information to the regional meeting, which had been called for in early May to consider the "needs of the people" and the "best method of procedure in the future." Any county not reporting would be presumed to need no further relief. This assembly was not intended to initiate direct action within the counties but to lay the needs of the area before the state government. The organizers, therefore, invited Governor Cushman K. Davis, or his representative, to attend.[6]

When the gathering convened (without the governor), delegates from Martin, Murray, Jackson, and Cottonwood counties articulated the problem: most farmers were poor when they settled on their land — the normal condition of newcomers, who comprised most of the population of the four counties. During the previous winter many had "exhaust[ed] almost every source for the means of living." Now further crop destruction seemed inevitable. Thousands who had not previously needed assistance would "be added to the list of destitute." Without help, many would be forced to leave their farms, including some who had fought during the war between the states. The delegates agreed that two possible solutions existed. Families could abandon their farms and live elsewhere until it was practical to return, or the committee could call on the United States Congress for an appropriation "sufficient to enable us to remain on our claims and renew our efforts. . . ." Not surprisingly, they favored the second alternative. They passed a resolution calling on Governor Davis to send a delegate to Washington to present the case and secure an appropriation. They also urged some provision for the protection of the settlers' land claims — both homestead and pre-emption — "should they be forced to leave them for a time to earn their living."[7]

At the suggestion of the governor, citizens of Martin County convened in late June to consider the needs of the county. With Davis' encouragement, the participants abandoned private relief committees and called on the county board of commissioners to assume the responsibilities of a central relief committee. The needy would not be added to the poor-relief rolls, but the commissioners, as elected officials, could bring more organization and respectability to the task of relief. They would act primarily as receivers and distributors of contributions coming in from outside the county. To draw maximum funds, the meeting authorized the commissioners to appoint one or more "solicitors" to plead their case.[8]

Commissioners throughout southwestern Minnesota headed relief efforts in mid-1874. Some, as in Martin County, distributed only what came from outside. Others drew on county revenues. The Brown County commissioners appropriated one thousand dollars to purchase food. The Nobles County board assigned "an amount not exceeding $2000" for immediate relief. Nobles County, like most of the area, did not have that much money available; therefore, the commissioners agreed to market bonds for up to the required amount, but sold only one thousand dollars worth. They also asked former Governor Stephen Miller, then president of the Southern Minnesota Railroad, to waive or at least reduce shipping costs for relief goods.[9]

The involvement of county commissioners did not mean that all

49

private efforts had ended. In Nobles County a group of individuals selected one citizen to solicit outside the county — outside the state, if necessary — to gather funds and promised to pay his expenses. This solicitor raised about twenty-one hundred dollars — some help, but still insufficient. In mid-October a public meeting convened to discuss the emergency conditions that winter would surely bring and called on the "charitable of our own state" and of the rest of the country, as well as the federal government, to come forward with assistance. The chairman was directed to seek official state aid. A final resolution requested the county commissioners to issue no more bonds to fund relief.[10]

Private groups and county commissioners faced similar, and enormous, problems in their attempts to diminish need. Raising money from individuals was not easy. As one observer noted, all the afflicted counties had an equal claim on people's charity, and when a county solicited funds for itself it encouraged "rivalry among the Beggers" and mistrust among the givers.[11]

Warren Smith, the Jackson County solicitor, complained from Milwaukee in late 1874 that the Martin County representative, A. C. Hand, had already tilled that part of Wisconsin so thoroughly that Smith's efforts proved difficult, unproductive, and "unpleasant." Moreover, Smith reported, he faced competition with representatives from other states. Men from Kansas and Nebraska had "plowed and scooped to the *bed rock*" the larger towns and cities in Wisconsin.[12]

The solicitor from Martin County, with whom Smith had competed, had himself met with only limited success. In the fall of 1874 he traveled to Ohio and Illinois as well as Wisconsin. Chinch bugs in northern Illinois had reduced crop yields there and left even sympathetic farmers with little to contribute. Merchants in all three states felt the effects of the depression that was gripping the country and could not offer much. Some who could afford to give questioned the propriety and sincerity of Hand's appeal. If such an emergency existed, they asked, why did the governor not act? Why did the state legislature not step in? Why was a lone representative from a single county asking for help from private citizens of another area? Such questions, too, kept contributions down. Hand raised less than eight hundred dollars during his travels.[13]

Sometimes the resentment of potential givers diminished the effectiveness of public appeals. According to a reporter, residents of

New York City, overwhelmed by demands at home, were "quite unable to do much for the unfortunate farmers of Nebraska, Kansas and other westerly regions." Farmers seemed to think, according to the correspondent, that New Yorkers had unlimited means. New Yorkers felt that no matter how generously they contributed they would be constantly besieged by requests from the West. "There seems to be always a miserable condition of things somewhere or other out there. Now it is Minnesota or Iowa; now it is Nebraska or Kansas; now it is some Southern state." Sharing their exasperation, the reporter wrote: "We have heard of famine, suffering and misery in Kansas at least half a dozen times during the past ten years." Why, in heaven's name, he wondered, did not the people of the West just leave that wretched area and go to Canada or Mexico or some other place? Or, even better, why did not the western farming classes help themselves and stop depending so heavily on the benevolent people of New York? The reporter concluded by stating, "It is humiliating to have them so constantly before us, passing round the hat." It is not clear, however, who found the experience humiliating, New Yorkers or westerners.[14]

Distribution of relief caused even worse problems. The single most significant one was that of limited funds. At best a county could help only those in the most severe straits. The Nobles County committee, for example, directed that only the "actually needy" be included among the eligible and that any who could support themselves, even when such support required personal sacrifice, be excluded from consideration. Watonwan County had about $350 to distribute among more than seventy families. On an average, each family received about four dollars, "a very small amt. towards keeping them until spring," lamented one committee member. Watonwan was not unusual in its limited resources.[15]

Delegates at the regional meeting estimated that approximately 1,425 families in Martin, Murray, Jackson, and Cottonwood counties needed relief. Additional stricken families — uncounted — resided in Nobles, Rock, Lyon, Redwood, Watonwan, and Brown counties. The participants agreed that to support a family for one year required almost two hundred dollars. The Martin County representative estimated that in his district alone at least 450 families — about 60 percent of the total county population — required some form of assistance. This would mean, he suggested, an expenditure of about ninety thousand dollars. The total revenue of Martin County in 1874 amounted to only $2,488, of which $498 was allocated for poor relief. Clearly, neither the county nor private committees could provide such enormous funds. The regional committee could not even guess where that much money would come from.[16]

Accusations against committee members proved to be another difficulty. One disgruntled Martin County citizen complained to Governor Davis that "wastage and stealing" occurred when private organizations administered relief. Neighbors and friends of members, he charged, often received more than their fair share. He thought that private distribution, even when conducted honestly and fairly, was vulnerable to suspicions of dishonesty. He urged public, county control.[17]

Responding to charges of favoritism, county committees in 1874 and 1875 took pains to ensure fair allotment of contributions. The Martin County commissioners received all relief goods and divided them among the townships. They allocated supplies on the basis of population — determined initially by names on the personal property assessment rolls and eventually by statements furnished by township officers of the number of families and of persons. Township committees handled individual distribution. These officials knew the people in their areas and could more accurately distinguish between the truly needy and the undeserving. Local committees had leeway to decide who needed help, but they were charged to make decisions "keeping the wishes of the donors in view" by giving only to the "most needy."[18]

Even these precautions did not prevent complaints of favoritism or of slights. One group suspected that another received more. An individual might believe that a neighbor got something extra. As a Murray County group charged: "The rest of the county it seems have had aid while this town has been left out in the cold and uncared for. . . ." Obviously county supervision did not resolve the problem of suspicions and accusations of unfairness. From Brown County, Governor Davis received a report that the commissioners had ignored people who lived away from the county seat. The correspondent stated that, according to the officials, "New Ulm is the County of Brown," and the little relief available went to those in and near New Ulm, the county seat. In reaction to this injustice, the "outsiders" formed their own distibuting unit and asked the governor to send assistance directly to them.

In another part of Brown County, a "Committee of Many Distressed Citizens" called a meeting to air their accusations and provide for their needs. The chairman requested that a representative of the governor attend and listen to the suggestions and complaints. They objected to county commissioners serving as distribution agents. "The office is to[o] high, and requires Constituants pets and favorites to get from them fat takes, enemies nothing." Participants at the meeting overwhelmingly approved resolutions charging the commissioners with neglect and calling for a separate committee to distribute aid. They charged that through "improper motives, political wire pulling, and false pride" the commissioners had not fully stated the needs of the county and bore the responsibility for its forfeiting its fair share. Therefore, the citizens requested that further assistance or indeed any further communication about relief be directed to them.[19]

One particularly assiduous critic was Edward F. Wade, town supervisor and relief chairman of West Cedar Township in Martin County. In December 1874 when West Cedar citizens' supplies were running low, Wade wrote that while people did not believe themselves purposely overlooked in the distribution of assistance, they observed that "the Lions share falls to those citizens living near the County Seat." Wade and his neighbors of West Cedar hoped that the governor could help them get their share.[20]

Fairmont, seat of Martin County, and West Cedar Township are about twenty miles apart — too far in 1875 for a one-day round trip. Notices of relief meetings normally circulated through the county newspaper, which was published in Fairmont. Where the paper did not circulate regularly or when weather and road conditions prevented its distribution, those who lived away from the county seat did not know what was going on. For example, the *Martin County Sentinel*, on September 4, 1874, announced a meeting in Fairmont on September 10 of the township relief committees. Its purpose was to arrange "for the distribution among the towns of the money and other articles in the hands of the county Committee." The announcement urged each town to send a representative who had information on the families in each township, as the size of the population determined the share of the allocation. This allowed only five days for the newspaper to get to West Cedar, for someone to compile a census (or at least some figures), and for the delegate to journey to Fairmont. Such a short time allowance forced speedy action by township officials and aroused the suspicions of West Cedar people, including Wade. Was this, he queried, evidence that county officials were intentionally trying to exclude the outliers?[21]

The commissioners may have lacked sensitivity to the problem of distance, but they tried to distribute help fairly. Between September 1874 and June 1875 they published in the *Sentinel* three reports that specified how relief had been allocated. Two of the accounts gave the information by township. The detail furnished suggests that the reason the commissioners published them was, at least in part, to protect themselves against accusations of partiality.[22]

Fairmont Township and the eight surrounding townships contained 54 percent of the total county population. Of the flour distributed, these nine townships received 52 percent — 2 percent less than their proportion of the population. Of the clothing dispensed, this group received 53 percent. The nine central townships were allotted 54 percent of the available money, which was their proportionate share. Fairmont Township, considered separately, indicates similar figures. It got less than its proportion of flour and of cash and clothing, exactly its share.

Only 2.8 percent of the county population resided in West Cedar Township; it received 4 percent of the flour and 2.8 percent of clothing and cash, apparently its fair share. West Cedar residents might, however, have argued that Fairmont Township — including as it did the town of Fairmont — should have had less, since presumably some of those residents were not farmers and, therefore, were not technically eligible for relief. Fairmont people might well have replied that whether or not they felt the direct effects of the grasshopper ravages, they did suffer indirect damages because of the lessened buying power of residents and the generally depressed economy that occurred when loss was so general.

Wade did not raise the only questions about Martin County distribution. In January the committee reported a stock of 782 pounds of flour. In June the committee stated that six hundred pounds had been on hand in January — an unexplained shrinkage of almost one-fourth. The suspicious could also question the reports themselves, the absence of itemized expenditures, and the vague categories such as, "Extra relief furnished different parties" or "Cash disbursements from Sept. 10 to January 1st, 1875, $775.40."[23]

Other evidence, too, raises questions about the manner of distribution. The people of Olmsted County in eastern Minnesota formed a relief committee and funneled their assistance primarily to

Martin County. In March 1875 they sent Mrs. E. Sherman to Fairmont "to assist the County Commissioners in the distribution of our supplies to the most needy. . . ." The commissioners offered her a less than cordial welcome and refused her help, "as they had their own plan of township distribution." Sherman filed a scathing report on that plan. She charged that it was unsystematic and disorderly and lacked careful management. Clothing received the previous July remained unopened. Most seriously, Sherman alleged that the commissioners "generally help themselves out of the best portion first." These were alarming indictments.[24]

To another critic who charged that the commissioners took pay for their services, the chairman, Thomas Curtis, replied that "to some extent" this was true. He justified it by listing the responsibilities the commissioners carried in organizing and assigning relief. "The necessity for keeping a book of receipts & expenditures the conducting of an extensive correspondence involving the writing of hundreds of letters compelled the Commissioners to hire a storehouse at Fairmont and keep one of their number in almost constant attendance." They believed it "no more than right" that whoever took on this duty should receive some pay, and he received the wages of a common day laborer. In over three months only about forty dollars had been expended for these services. None of the commissioners was rich, Curtis wrote, and if anyone would do the job for less, they would certainly consider his application. So far no one had stepped forward.[25]

Apparently nothing ever came of these various accusations, and the Olmsted committee complained no further. Possibly theft or fraud occurred, but it cannot be proven. County governments remained the primary receivers, distributors, and supervisors. Wade's intercession, however, benefited the people of West Cedar. His trip to see the governor in January met with success: one hundred dollars from the state relief committee plus a box of clothing and a barrel of beef. In Wade's words, "it proved the best and most efficient aid we have received and more than we had received altogether previously." Thus, West Cedar received not only its fair share from the county, but also extra from the state as well.[26]

One possible explanation for the seeming unfairness of distribution resulted from the allocation being based on population size. Although the county as a whole suffered, a number of people salvaged part of their crops. Others could support themselves adequately without resort to county assistance. A system that depended on numbers of people encouraged padding the figures and discouraged concentration on the most needy. The limited amount of assistance available demanded a more careful measure of destitution. One did not materialize.

In the summer of 1875 many people enjoyed a reprieve. The grasshoppers formed, according to a poetic county historian, a "ragamuffin Falstaffin army, compared with that of . . . 1874." The commissioner of statistics reported, "The average as well as the aggregate production of most crops was good in 1875, notwithstanding continued grasshopper injuries in the west. . . ." In Martin County, for example, losses decreased dramatically. In 1874 the settlers lost over eleven thousand acres of wheat; in 1875 under one thousand acres were damaged. Of the counties afflicted in both years only four sustained greater losses to wheat acreage in 1875 than in 1874. This decline resulted in a marked decrease in relief activity. In Rock County the combination of increased crop yields and a mild winter meant that "very little relief was needed." Similar conditions prevailed over much of southwestern Minnesota. Upon publication of the final report of the commissioners in 1875, the *Martin County Sentinel* editorialized: "In all probability Martin county will never again be compelled to ask assistance. There are but few people in the county but what, by industry and perseverance, can take care of themselves and they will hereafter be expected to do it."[27]

During the respite, officials turned their attention from relief to prevention. County groups organized to declare war on the grasshoppers. At the request of a mass meeting of citizens, the Meeker County board of commissioners met in June 1875 "to take some action in regard to the extermination of grasshoppers." The board offered a bounty of five dollars per bushel of grasshoppers caught between June 15 and 21. Six other counties and some towns followed suit. Officials in the town of Le Sueur estimated that there were about one hundred bushels of grasshoppers within the village limits and offered twenty cents per quart. In a few days the bounty had to be reduced because the number caught so exceeded the estimate. Blue Earth County officials acted similarly, allocating money to pay for three thousand bushels. Over nine hundred were caught in three days and nearly sixteen thousand bushels in all. The seven counties paid almost seventy-seven thousand dollars in bounties. The counties that offered bounties were among the older and better developed of those hit by grasshoppers. The drain on the treasuries was enormous. These counties could not afford such expenditures, but they tried to pay them. Newer, less populated ones could not begin to do so. Bounties served the dual purpose of destroying the insects and providing work for the needy, but when the payments threatened to bankrupt the counties, the practice was quickly abandoned.[28]

In the summer of 1876 the reprieve ended abruptly. The pests returned to renew and increase their damage. In November the voters elected John S. Pillsbury governor. He made it clear that he valued self-help and that he discounted organized assistance. During his administration, county commissioners held only marginal responsibility for relief. They did not again solicit, collect, or distribute it. Thus the phase of assistance in which county governments or private local committees were largely accountable effectively ended with the election of the new governor.

5

The State Steps In

The grasshopper years were not the first during which Minnesota farmers needed help. In 1871 hail and prairie fires damaged crops in scattered areas. Governor Horace Austin first called for private contributions for the needy and then asked the legislature to act. When private assistance failed, he argued, the state had a responsibility to step in. The legislature refused to appropriate subsistence relief for destitute farmers but agreed to offer them seed grain.[1]

The legislators established careful guidelines for the disbursement of seed money. In areas where crops were destroyed "to an extent sufficient to cause distress," the boards of county commissioners were to meet with citizens who had sustained uninsured losses and could present sworn statements of them. The boards determined the legitimacy of each claim and then submitted written reports to the governor about the applicants, including name, age, marital status, number of children, acres destroyed, acres prepared for seeding, and any assets.

When in January 1873 a severe blizzard left seventy settlers dead, an uncounted number more injured, and thousands of farm animals destroyed, Governor Austin recommended that the legislature — then sitting in session — take "prompt action to provide temporary relief." The legislators appropriated five thousand dollars "for the relief of persons requiring medical, surgical, and other aid" and assigned the money to the governor to distribute. They also called on Congress to "permit widows who lost their husbands in the late snow storm to receive patents of Their homesteads forthwith."[2]

The governor, to help in allocating the five thousand dollars, asked county officials to "provide the whole truth" about losses. Then he allowed fifty dollars to each of the widows, twenty-five dollars to individuals who were injured, and an undetermined amount for medical services. Going beyond the letter of the law, Austin also allotted money for those who had lost and could not replace their only cow or team.[3]

These actions revealed that sometimes state officials accepted the principle of government responsibility for the needy. The manner in which the aid was given, however, suggests an ambivalent attitude toward the recipients. If the cause and effect of a crisis, such as a blizzard, were life threatening and obvious, then the state allowed the governor to act without dictating specific terms of the aid. When, however, the cause of the need was agricultural, the legislature refused immediate relief until applicants had been carefully screened. The state government, unaccustomed to the role of almoner, seemed unsure whether the recipients were "paupers," and therefore to be suspected, or whether they were disaster victims, and thus undeserving of suspicion.

In 1873 the first people who met the needs of grasshopper-stricken farmers were not state officials, but private citizens. An appeal by the Cottonwood County Relief Committee fell into the hands of Henry Hastings Sibley. The grasshopper victims could not have found in the entire state a more highly regarded spokesman for their cause.

Few men inspired as much respect in Minnesota during the second half of the nineteenth century as did General Sibley. Born in Detroit, Michigan, in 1811, he moved to Mendota in 1834 to take charge of the American Fur Company post. He served two terms as territorial delegate to Congress and in 1858 became the first governor of the new state of Minnesota. During the Dakota War of 1862 he led a force of fifteen hundred men that played a crucial role in ending the hostilities and freeing white captives. These actions made Sibley something of a hero. By the early 1870s he had retired to more peaceful pursuits. He helped organize the St. Paul Chamber of Commerce and served as its president. He was a founder and later president of the Minnesota Historical Society, a member of the University of Minnesota Board of Regents, and board chairman of the St. Paul and Sioux City Railroad. Sibley reigned as one of the grand old men of Minnesota, and he exercised wide influence.[4]

When Sibley received the Cottonwood County appeal he knew precisely where to garner assistance. He turned first to the St. Paul Chamber of Commerce, to which he sent a copy of the plea and a report of equal suffering in other counties, writing, "I am convinced that properly organized efforts, under the direction of the Chamber of Commerce, will be attended with entire success in eliciting contributions from our citizens in money, or in food or clothing." He "trusted" that the chamber would take "speedy action." It did by calling a public meeting "to provide means for the relief of our fellow citizens . . . [who] are now suffering for want of the necessaries of life."[5]

A special committee called the sparsely attended meeting to order, introduced reports on the emergency, and suggested possible forms of action. Sibley announced that Governor Austin would recommend that the legislature appropriate seed grain but believed that immediate relief in the form of money, food, clothing, and other supplies, should come from "voluntary and personal contributions." The chamber took up the challenge. They agreed that this case called for the "active sympathy of the charitable," no less than had the Chicago fire of recent memory when St. Paul contributed twenty thousand dollars. The group appointed one committee to draft an appeal and another, of which Sibley was chairman, to collect funds. Because the need was acute, the committees began work immediately.[6]

The next day the appeals committee published its plea, asking for "immediate sympathy and assistance" and requesting local pastors to read the appeal to their congregations on the following Sunday. The other committee appointed ward-level collection teams in St. Paul and called on the "authorities" in six of the larger Minnesota towns — Stillwater, Hastings, Red Wing, Winona, Rochester, and Owatonna — to co-operate in this "charitable work."[7]

The message fell on only mildly sympathetic ears in these towns. Private citizens in Owatonna formed committees to collect contributions and prevailed on local pastors to read the appeal from their pulpits. They also called on the state's legislators to appropriate money "to meet the wants of this unfortunate portion of her citizens." This flurry of activity, however, resulted in a total collection of something under one hundred dollars in Owatonna. Other towns sent larger amounts — ranging from $165 to $300 — raised among the local population. Only in Winona did the county commissioners dip into their treasury for a donation. In general, the bulk of the private relief effort was left to the people of the capital city.[8]

With no small measure of civic pride and boosterism, the *St. Paul Daily Pioneer* reported on the money raised: "St. Paul is a whole-souled, generous city, even if we do say it. She never yet has turned

Cushman K. Davis, governor of Minnesota in 1874–76, while sympathetic to the sufferers, insisted on a strict accounting of all relief goods and money disbursed.

Mary Carpenter worried about surviving on the frontier in the wake of the grasshopper ravages when she wrote to her Aunt Martha, July 10, 1873.

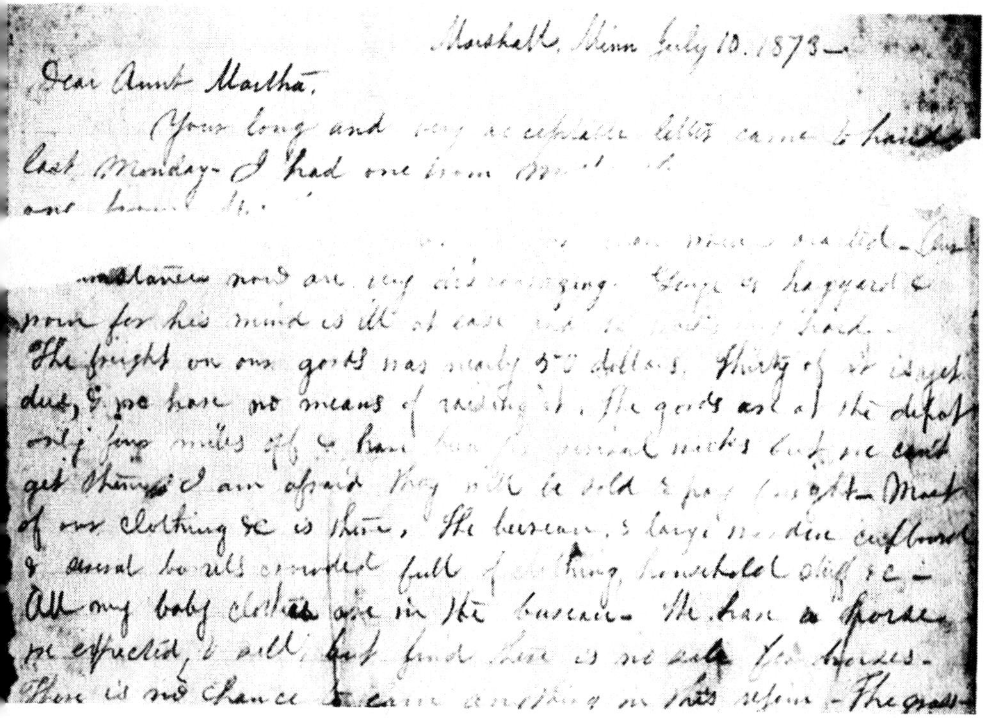

Marshall, Minn July 10. 1873—

Dear Aunt Martha,

Your long and very acceptable letter came to hand last Monday— I had one from [illegible] one from [illegible]

[illegible] circumstances now are very discouraging. George is haggard & worn for his mind is ill at ease [illegible]— The freight on our goods was nearly 50 dollars. Thirty of it is yet due, & we have no means of raising it. The goods are at the depot only four miles off & have been for several weeks but we can't get them & I am afraid they will be sold to pay freight— Most of our clothing &c is there, the bureau, a large wooden cupboard & several boxes crowded full of clothing household stuff &c— All my baby clothes are in the bureau— We have a horse we expected to sell, but find there is no sale for horses. There is no chance to earn anything in this region— The grass

STATE OF MINNESOTA,
County of *Martin* } ss. *G. W. Anson*

having been duly sworn, deposes that he is a resident of the town of *Manyaska* county of *Martin*
Minnesota. That your petitioner is deserving of relief under the provisions of the act of January 26, 1875; that your petitioner
is wholly without means.

(Sign.) *Geo. W. Anson*

Subscribed and sworn to this *second* day of *March* A. D. 1875, before me.

J. C. Everett

We approve the above application. *B. M. Thomas* *Justice of the Peace*

W. T. Harnden

John S. Schultz

(This approval to be signed by township Supervisors, or by a majority of the County Commissioners, when there are no supervisors or no township organization in the town.

*Applicants for relief had to sign a pauper's oath swearing that they
were "wholly without means" and therefore "deserving of relief."
Four witnesses attested to the truth of the oath.*

*Shortly after swearing he had no financial resources whatsoever, this
petitioner received two dollars worth of goods — pork (about ten
pounds), matches, saleratus (baking soda), and molasses.*

Received of C. K. DAVIS, Governor of Minnesota, per
T. S. Custis Commission *$2.00*

on this *10th* day of *March* 1875, the following articles, deliv-
ered to me under the Act of 1875, appropriating money to relieve the sufferers upon the
frontier:

QUANTITY.		Dollars.	Cents.
	Pork	1	13
	Match		25
	Saleratus		10
	Molass		52
	Total,	2	00

(Signature) *Geo. W. Anson*

Henry H. Sibley in 1870 shortly before Governor Davis called upon him to co-ordinate relief efforts for the victims of the grasshopper plague.

Sibley kept a careful account of the money entrusted to him. Most of the funds disbursed went to county agents for direct relief and to railroads for tickets and freightage of goods.

				Dr.	Cr.
1875		Amounts brought forward		4.392 59	2.096 62
Feb. 3	By Cash paid Phinney Rock Co. 10. Mrs. Jenney, Martin Co. 5				
	B. F. Renn Nobles Co. 15	Ch 52			30 "
8	" " " Comm'rs Jackson Co.	53			200 "
9	" " " L. C. Clark for poor in Watonwan Co.	54			200 "
"	" " " Comm'rs. Rock Co. 55-200 & 300 15th	56			500 "
19	" " " St. P. & S. C. R. R. Co. "3 fare N. Smith Worthington	57			4 50
20	" " " Wm. M. Davis Chr. Borden Murray Co.	58			50 "
24	" " " J. R. Dalton Center Creek Martin Co.	59			20 "
25	" " " 2 hf. fare tickets to Worthington	60			8 90
26	" " " St. P. & S. C. R. R. Co. for freight	61			71 57
"	" " " J. H. Reaney to refund advances	62			23 01

John S. Pillsbury during his first term as governor of Minnesota, 1876–78, coped with the final years of the grasshopper plagues. He refused to undermine the moral fiber of the poor by giving them hand-outs.

Mahala Fisk Pillsbury, wife of the governor, shared her husband's ideas about charity.

State relief money financed this pamphlet. It was designed to show that if the farmers just worked hard enough, they could rid the state of grasshoppers.

Applicant Number 66 in Martin County received ten bushels of seed wheat. He could expect to plant seven and one-half acres and, with luck, harvest 135 bushels (less seed for next year) that would bring in one dollar per bushel. Minimum yearly maintenance for a family of four was estimated at two hundred dollars.

INFORMATION

CONCERNING THE

GRASSHOPPER,

—OR—

ROCKY MOUNTAIN LOCUST.

It is sought by the publication of this pamphlet to place in the hands of every farmer living in the country adjacent to the SOUTHERN MINNESOTA RAILROAD, where the Grasshoppers have appeared, the most trustworthy information in regard to the methods which have been employed with the most success in checking or preventing their ravages.

Of the very valuable report of the committee appointed by Governor Davis to investigate and report upon this subject, and from which these extracts have been made, only 5,000 copies were printed—not a sufficient number to reach every person interested, and it is hoped that this partial re-print will, in a measure, supply the deficiency.

A copy of Governor Pillsbury's proclamation, containing many useful and valuable suggestions, is appended.

There can be little doubt that the energetic application of the means herein recommended, will be rewarded by very great, if not complete success.

EVERYTHING DEPENDS UPON EARLY ORGANIZATION, HEARTY CO-OPERATION AND PROMPT ACTION.

Printed for the SOUTHERN MINNESOTA RAILROAD,
BY THE LA CROSSE REPUBLICAN AND LEADER,
September, 1876.

SEED GRAIN CONTRACT.

$10.00

No. 66

FAIRMONT, MARTIN COUNTY, MINN.

March 23d 1878.

For and in consideration of 10 bushels of seed Wheat and —— bushels of seed ———————————— received from the State of Minnesota, under and by virtue of "An Act to furnish and distribute seed grain for sufferers from grasshopper ravages, approved February 13th, 1878," I hereby promise to pay to the said State the sum of Ten (10) Dollars, the cost of said seed grain; and agree that said sum shall be taxable against my real and personal property, the same to be levied by the County Auditor of said County, and the said tax to be collected by virtue of the laws of this State; and I hereby further agree that said sum so levied shall be a first lien upon my crop of grain, raised each year, until said tax is paid.

Wm P McGhan

Attest:
J A Armstrong

Post Office address Cedarville

Auditor of said County.

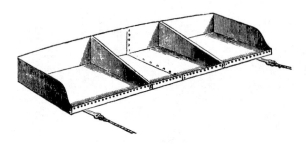

Several farmers created simple hopperdozers from a piece of sheet metal that they coated with coal tar and dragged through an infested field. At each end of the field, the mess was scraped into a bonfire and the metal recoated for another trip.

For several months running, a merchant in Fairmont advertised his goods at "grasshopper prices" (Martin County Sentinel, *July 10, 1874).*

Manufacturers developed expensive, sophisticated horse-driven hopperdozers, but impoverished farmers could not afford to buy them.

a deaf ear to a cry for aid where it was needed and her prompt and liberal response to the appeal . . . is only another evidence of her big-hearted method of relieving the deserving needy." From local businessmen alone the committee had collected over six hundred dollars in less than two hours and, the story reported, the solicitors had "not met with a repulse in a single instance." Those unable to give money often gave food or clothing. In three days the chamber collected almost twelve hundred dollars in cash, plus at least that much more in pledges, and had already sent over one thousand dollars to the frontier counties.[9]

Sibley's committee made arrangements for distribution by organizing relief committees in counties that had none. He asked "reliable and true" men in the afflicted areas "to whose hands was committed the duty of ministering the wants of the needy citizens" to help the chamber determine how to proportion the contributions. Although local committees performed their work "diligently, faithfully, and equitably," according to Sibley, the chamber nonetheless employed a St. Paul man to oversee distribution of the first large shipment of goods. In late December, at Sibley's request, former Governor Stephen Miller toured the southwestern counties to report on conditions and to establish additional committees where needed. In Murray County he interviewed several "leading men" and suggested how they might organize to help the destitute. Then he moved on to Mankato. Citizens there were doing nothing, and he hoped to set up a plan for giving. Meeting with success, Miller reported that Mankato "will make our people a handsome donation."[10]

Sibley capitalized on his position as board chairman of the St. Paul and Sioux City Railroad to further the relief effort. He pledged the road to carry the supplies free of charge. By himself he collected almost one thousand dollars by asking each nonresident board member to contribute at least one hundred dollars.[11]

Primary credit for the efforts of the St. Paul Chamber of Commerce and of citizens lay with Sibley. Through his active leadership, his continuing commitment, and the use of his connections, Sibley ensured that the needy would not go hungry. In all, the chamber collected over six thousand dollars in cash and a "very large donation" of clothing, bedding, provisions, and wood. Despite all efforts, however, private citizens could not satisfy even the most pressing demands, and the state, of necessity, had to act.[12]

Governor Austin remained in office until January 1874. In his

final message to the legislature he laid out the plight of the settlers:
"The loss of the harvest upon which they depended for the year's food
and the means of procuring clothing and other necessaries," he
stated, "has left many of them in a state of absolute destitution and
impending suffering, if not relieved by the hand of charity." He
reiterated his hope for a generous private response but maintained
that if donations could not satisfy the need, then the state must step
in. State government bore a positive responsibility to provide the
means for obtaining seed grain, he declared, but "Among a people
so well off as ours, this is all that the State as such should be called
upon to do." Thus, during Austin's last months in office, all assistance was left to private charity.[13]

Cushman K. Davis, who succeeded Austin as governor in early
1874, did not entirely share Austin's views. In his inaugural address
Davis offered thanks for the abundance of the previous year but
noted that, through no fault of their own, many Minnesotans did not
partake of that abundance. As the victims of a calamity that "no
vigilance can guard against," the suffering farmers should "become
the objects of our immediate action." Davis spoke specifically about
the state's responsibility: "The government, acting through counties
and cities, has from the beginning extended a liberal charity towards
individual sufferers. Here, however, is an instance where the sufferers and the inhabitants of entire communities are identical. They
cannot as communities help themselves." He asked the legislature to
act immediately and liberally by appropriating direct relief — seed
grain could come later. The state should act, he argued, out of both
humanitarian concern and self-interest. Minnesota's future rested on
the fate of these needy settlers and others like them. They, argued
Davis, "have undertaken amid many privations to extend the in-
habited and productive area of our State; they are new comers,
whose success will have a powerful influence upon immigration."
To sustain these people was to promote the interests of the state; to
ignore them was to threaten its welfare.[14]

Sibley, too, appealed to the legislature. He recommended an
appropriation "sufficient to provide for the wants of the suffering
settlers" and estimated that at least six hundred families needed
complete support through the winter while an untold number of
others required partial support "to enable them to pass safely
through."[15]

The legislators responded in several ways. As a first gesture in a joint resolution they asked the federal government to extend payment deadlines for settlers on pre-emption lands. Then they extended by several months (through the harvest) the deadline for payment of personal property taxes in only nine grasshopper counties. In late January 1874 they appropriated five thousand dollars "to aid the destitute settlers upon the frontier." Like the 1873 relief bill for snowstorm victims, the 1874 legislation allowed the governor to disburse the allocation "at his discretion." Finally, the representatives turned their attention to providing seed for the destitute farmers. In early March Davis signed into law an appropriation of twenty-five thousand dollars "or so much thereof as may be necessary" for seed grain. The legislation stipulated that no one family could receive more than thirty-five dollars, but beyond that left the governor the "full care, management and disbursement of said sum." Thus, Davis assumed personal responsibility for the distribution of a total of thirty thousand dollars. He faced the difficult task of stretching that money to meet the needs of many.[16]

Davis acted quickly to organize the distribution of the relief funds. On January 30 he met with state representatives from the grasshopper district to determine who should be responsible for distributing the money locally. Rather than working through the county commissioners, he appointed "reliable and active men in the more important localities" to serve as general relief committees. To forestall any accusations of mismanagement or fraud, Davis asked these citizens to serve without compensation.[17]

To guarantee a "fair and equal distribution" of the limited funds, Davis issued specific instructions — a list of "dos" and "don'ts." He directed the committees not to provide seed (to be taken care of later), spirits, tobacco, coffee, tea, sugar, blankets, or clothing. Disbursements should be in the form of supplies — not cash. Settlers who owned "surplus stock" were not to receive aid; they should sell their animals and care for themselves. Among the "dos" were instructions to visit the localities that claimed need and to assist only those "whom you may know to be deserving, from personal inspection. . . ." Davis asked that careful receipts be kept — both from merchants and recipients. Then, by March 1, the committees were to provide detailed reports, including names and addresses of recipients and an exact accounting of what each received.[18]

These stipulations governed what in most cases were small amounts of aid. The Rock County committee, for example, received only $390. It allocated this sum to provide for forty-one families, an average of about $9.50 for each. Jackson County received $640, more than any other county, but it also had the largest number of needy. The committee helped 147 families, giving each an average of about four dollars. The Martin County committee received $360 and assisted sixty-four heads of households.[19]

These small amounts did not satisfy the need in the afflicted counties. While Davis no doubt wanted to promote the best use of the limited legislative appropriation, his careful instructions suggest an underlying suspicion of the recipients. Davis assumed that the relief committees would handle the money better than could the beneficiaries themselves, apparently fearing that the needy would squander cash. He probably expected the ineligible to apply for assistance; therefore, he required that each applicant be personally investigated. These precautions seem out of proportion to the amounts of relief available. They suggest a tendency to think of the disaster victims as "poor people" with all of the personal and moral weaknesses attributed to them in the nineteenth century.

Destitution persisted after the distribution of the state funds. To keep informed of the situation, Governor Davis sent a representative, George Overton, from St. Paul to survey the grasshopper counties. Overton wrote from Cottonwood County, "There is no mistake about the condition of these people, and they will have to be helped until next harvest." Already 114 families in the county needed aid and "new cases of destitution are being reported every day." In Jackson County Overton found an equally dismal situation. Reports had not been exaggerated. Although the state allocation temporarily met the need, more money would be required eventually. In Nobles County Overton discovered that the people "will need more relief funds than any point I've visited." He sent a different report from Rock County, where the farm families "are better off than any on the line of my travels." In fact, he reported, they could have gotten along satisfactorily without any state money. "They don't need what they have got and they laugh at the idea amongst themselves for having got their share of 'Government Grab' as they call it. . . ."[20]

Overton's report raised a furor. Davis immediately fired off a letter to the Rock County Relief Committee requesting an explanation. P. J. Kniss, the chairman, responded, vehemently denying the accusations. Only those who had been turned down would make such an allegation, he believed, and they would do so out of anger, not from a fair appraisal of the need. One of those who had been denied had threatened to "*bust this whole thing up*." No doubt, according to Kniss, the misinformation came through jealousy. Davis also received other letters from Rock County. One group of men swore to the need and even volunteered to pay for a canvass of the county made by some trusted associate of the governor. Overton's report must have worried Davis, who was accountable for the money. Revengeful rumors also worried county officials, who stretched meager amounts as far as possible and still could not help all those in need. And, they reinforced the suspicions already held by many about the inadvisability of state assistance. All of Davis' careful planning could not prevent stories — even when obviously false — of "government grabs" from occurring.[21]

Overton also investigated citizen's complaints against the relief committees. A group of Lyon County settlers charged that the committee had ignored them even though they were in "great need and require[d] immediate relief." He found this charge entirely justified, for many had sold all of their salable property to buy food. Another man complained that, contrary to the governor's instructions, the committee had required him to sell his last team of oxen, "leaving him without means of transportation or of putting in crops next Season." Overton found this complaint true as well. In such cases Davis by-passed the committees and sent relief directly to the victims, but normally he left primary responsibility with the local groups, which, in general, were "well organized, energetic and working harmoniously." What is surprising is not that complaints surfaced but that so few occurred. The very scarcity of the charges attests to the care that local committees exercised in a situation likely to cause jealousy, desperation, and real inequities.[22]

Distribution of the immediate relief appropriation was easy, compared to the allocation of the seed-grain money. Instead of working exclusively through county citizens, Davis selected a three man committee. The members were all well-known, prominent citizens whose reputations placed them above suspicion. As the *St. Paul Daily Pioneer* noted, "The high character of each and all of the commissioners is a certain guarantee that the fund will be carefully and honestly distributed." The committee included David Day, Richard W. Johnson, and Stephen Miller. Day, a physician and long-time Minnesota resident, had served in the territorial legislature. Johnson, a West Point graduate and a major general in the Civil

71

War, had served at Fort Snelling for almost twenty years. Miller had been a lieutenant colonel of the First Minnesota Volunteer Infantry in the Civil War, was active in the Dakota War, and had served as both state legislator and governor. In 1874 Miller worked for Sibley and the St. Paul and Sioux City Railroad as superintendent of the company's land interests in southern Minnesota.[23]

Davis also asked George C. Chamberlin, former county auditor and state legislator and currently editor of the *Jackson Republican*, to serve, but Chamberlin declined. He would aid in any other capacity, he wrote, but if the duties would require him "to decide who is to have a portion of such wheat I desire that some other party may do that little thing." This thankless task was bound to make the commissioners the center of contentious argument. "An angel from Heaven could not suit the cusses who are clamoring for seed grain and other donations," Chamberlin stated, "so please select some person nearer even than angels to the Almighty in purity for that job. . . ." Chamberlin accurately predicted the dissension that was to surround the distribution of seed.[24]

The seed wheat commissioners met first in mid-March and agreed to purchase seed at $1.00 to $1.10 per bushel from elevators and warehouses both in St. Paul and along the line of the St. Paul and Sioux City Railroad. The 12 to 13 percent per bushel transportation costs led the commissioners to buy seed located as near as possible to the distribution points. Wrangling first arose over the decision to purchase only wheat. Some people believed that wheat offered only food for the pests and would prove a waste of money. Others believed that wheat would not provide food for the hungry settlers quickly enough. But the commissioners did not alter their plans.[25]

They based their apportionment on "information received . . . by letter and personal conference with the county authorities." The requests totaled over sixty thousand bushels. The commissioners had funds to supply less than one-third of the demand. They drew up careful distribution guidelines that "should be observed as far as practicable." Grain would be delivered, they directed, only when the applicant could provide a sworn statement of need validated by a justice of the peace. When the local board members did not personally know the applicant, they could require "additional proof . . . before his claim is allowed." They specified that the grain was to be used only as seed — not as food. The commissioners decided that the normal allotment should be under fifteen bushels, and in no case would one person receive more than twenty bushels, which was a limit lower than that provided by the legislation. Such small amounts could give a farmer only a start and certainly would not replace the wheat lost the previous year. At the rate of a bushel and a half of seed per acre, an estimate supplied by the commissioners, the average farmer could plant no more than ten acres with the seed furnished. The *St. Paul Daily Pioneer* applauded the allocation and found this amount "sufficient to give bread to the frontier" — the most that the farmers could expect. The farmers may have disagreed.[26]

Some county organizations imposed even stricter regulations. The Lyon County committee issued rules to be followed "WITHOUT VARIATION," stipulating that only those "absolutely destitute of seed wheat," with no means of obtaining it, and with ground proper for wheat could receive seed. They further stated that only one person in each family was eligible and no single person, except a widow or widower with a family, could receive seed. Finally, the Lyon County rules, more restrictive than the state's, limited the allotment to no more than six bushels per person. In a concluding passage somewhat out of harmony with the strict rules, the instructions voiced the hope of the relief committee that the distributors, "prompted by a generous public spirit, will be active in doing good toward their more unfortunate neighbors." These narrow guidelines made sure that each eligible applicant received something, but they did not afford much room for the exercise of a generous public spirit.[27]

By the end of March virtually all of the relief and seed funds had been expended, but serious need still existed. Davis continued to get pleas for help, and to Sibley came "daily application from the frontier counties for additional aid." Davis responded as best as he could from what little remained of state relief funds; Sibley "judiciously distributed" what was left of private contributions. Both feared, however, that many settlers would continue to suffer. They knew of nothing more that they could do. Farmers now had to wait, plant what crops they could, and hope that the grasshoppers would not renew their assaults.[28]

Davis did not limit his involvement to requesting aid from the legislature. In the spring of 1874 he began gathering information about grasshoppers, for like farmers and most entomologists, he knew little about the Rocky Mountain locust. He called on residents in every county that had been afflicted in 1873 and asked each the same questions. Were the hoppers hatching? In great numbers? Had the cold weather or any parasites damaged the eggs? Had the grasshoppers arrived in 1873 fully grown? Had any eggs hatched in the fall? Did the young fly away upon hatching? His queries reflect a desperate hope that somehow the scourge would be lifted from the land. But they also indicate the dearth of common knowledge about the basic habits of the grasshoppers.[29]

To these questions and to another set that Davis sent out later in the spring, he received distressing answers. Through the spring and summer of 1874 more and more farmers watched their crops fail. Where crops had been destroyed in 1873, settlers needed immediate help, and as a result of the 1874 losses, Davis knew, thousands of new victims would require relief eventually.

The governor ignored numerous requests to call a special legislative session during the summer or fall of 1874. But he realized that the "undirected promptings" of private charity could not meet the crisis. He developed a plan that he hoped would have immediate and substantial results and that combined private and public spheres. First he appealed officially for private contributions. Next he set up a state-wide relief fund and appointed a committee of businessmen and public officials to collect and allocate the donations. He proposed that county commissioners, rather than private citizens, handle local distribution of the nongovernmental assistance. Finally, he sent his private secretary to visit the suffering counties so that he himself could keep close watch on conditions.[30]

In a strongly worded appeal, Davis turned to the Patrons of Husbandry. Destitution that had "no parallel in our history as a state" gripped settlers in southwest Minnesota. Women and children suffered from lack of food and clothing. Farmers had already mortgaged stock and implements and could do no more. The "time for silence" had passed, Davis announced, and the "time for prompt and liberal action" had arrived. People needed the immediate assistance of the Grange. The resources of the Grange had not gone untapped in 1873, but its efforts were sporadic and scattered. A few branches made donations from their treasuries; others asked members to contribute or to collect from neighbors. Davis believed that the farmers' organization could and should do more.[31]

The *St. Paul Daily Pioneer* seconded Davis' request, noting that the Minnesota Grange, with its more than six hundred local branches and twenty-five thousand members, was "the most powerful organization that exists, whether considered in point of numbers or wealth and influence." City dwellers—merchants, mechanics, and laborers—had contributed generously, although they themselves faced economic depression. Now it was time, the paper editorialized, for those farmers on whom prosperity smiled to act on the benevolent principles upon which the order rested. What neither Davis nor the *Daily Pioneer* mentioned was the growing political strength of the Minnesota Grange. Ignatius Donnelly's and George I. Parsons' disagreements about the organization's political dimension had caused rifts within the membership. While Davis' appeal no doubt rested on humanitarian concerns, he might also have wanted to exploit the dissension by showing himself the farmers' true friend and weakening the move toward a third party. In any case, the Grange did represent a major source of potential assistance, one that should have been affected by news of destitute farm families.[32]

Several Granges responded swiftly. In amounts of five dollars to twenty dollars, local organizations showed their concern. Throughout the summer months they contributed more than three hundred dollars, a small sum that reflected primarily the tightness of cash rather than the stinginess of the Grangers. Most of their contributions came in the form of food—particularly wheat.

Davis could have timed his appeal somewhat better. His circular reached most farmers before harvest when they had little to give. One group assured Davis that it would do what it could immediately after harvest, but "just now our Graineries are empty." Another Grange agreed to assess its members two bushels of wheat for every one hundred bushels they raised. Yet other groups promised to try to raise money in their districts, as they themselves could not offer much. The National Grange responded somewhat more generously, sending two thousand dollars for relief.[33]

While the combined contributions of all the Grangers may have been generous, their efforts represented only a minor part of the assistance. Their later claim that "actual starvation must have resulted but for the nationwide Grange response" can surely be chalked up to organizational pride and exaggeration. In fact, it is surprising that a group dedicated to relieving the social and economic maladies of the farmers did so little.[34]

Davis also directed a letter to the board of commissioners in each county outside the distressed region. He had appealed to the Grangers' sympathies for other farmers; he couched his request to the commissioners in more pragmatic terms. The afflicted areas represented a vital part of the state's wealth, he argued, and the true valuation of their taxable real and personal property exceeded $4 million. This natural calamity threatened the "very existence of this property," the people themselves, and "all of their beneficial relations to the State. . . ." The people of Minnesota, he continued, could either offer assistance or they could allow those settlers to abandon their lands, causing the state enormous losses in population and property. The value of the region would be cancelled "as absolutely as if it were burned up. . . ." Both Christian charity and economic wisdom demanded that citizens assist to the limit of their abilities. Davis, therefore, asked the boards to make relief appropriations out of their county treasuries.[35]

Ramsey County — of which St. Paul is the seat — took the lead in responding. In early July, Davis and Sibley met with the board of commissioners to define the case. This extraordinary misfortune, Davis told them, had grown to an extent that "it was not in the power of private charity to alleviate"; Sibley affirmed flatly that without immediate assistance people would die. The board allotted five thousand dollars — a contribution as large as the total state appropriation the previous January. Davis worked particularly hard to get this first, substantial gift. He wanted to provide an example, as well as some pressure, to the other counties.[36]

Some counties proved impervious to pleas, pressure, and appeals to civic pride. Davis personally attended the Hennepin County commissioners' meeting in Minneapolis in mid-July. Hennepin County as the most populous county of the state should, Davis argued, give at least as much as Ramsey had. He explained that he could not apply state funds without legislative approval, and the expense of a special session made that prohibitive. Thus, he stated, "it remains for the people to make an appropriation for the relief of this suffering." His appeals, as well as urgings by prominent Minneapolis citizens, including the mayor, fell on deaf ears. The commissioners, convinced that such an appropriation would be illegal, refused to make a contribution. A group of private citizens, angered by this decision, stepped in and pledged five thousand dollars from their own pockets. The Hennepin County commissioners' action must have greatly disappointed Davis, particularly when Wright and Brown counties followed suit. Moreover, private citizens of these counties did not offer personal contributions to compensate for their commissioners' decisions. Crow Wing County commissioners were not concerned about the legality of an appropriation; they simply lacked enough money in the treasury for a contribution. They did agree, however, to take the governor's appeal to the Crow Wing County citizens and to encourage private donations. Houston County responded, but instead of adding their money to the general relief fund they sent almost one thousand dollars directly to the Martin County commissioners. No other counties made appropriations. In all, county governments donated about eleven thousand dollars — a bonanza in comparison with other sources, but not enough.[37]

To direct the state relief committee, Davis appointed Henry H. Sibley, the obvious choice. The group included William H. Dike, a Faribault businessman; Lorenzo Hoyt, a farmer and legislator; Ebenezer Ayers, another farmer and two-term legislator; and John S. Pillsbury, a prominent Minneapolis businessman and legislator. These appointees, like those of the previous winter, were solid, respected citizens, above reproach and suspicion. From July through December 1874 they acted as the primary agents for overseeing, collecting, and funneling contributions. On Davis' suggestion, they made distribution a matter of "official duty" and worked exclusively through the elected boards of county commissioners in the afflicted areas.[38]

The state relief committee did not want to appeal to the federal government or to other states in any official capacity, believing that Minnesota "could well afford to care for their [sic] own distressed citizens." They considered such an appeal unnecessary and, more importantly, they worried that widely circulated information about devastation in the southwestern counties would injure the state. Such damage would offset any benefits realized from out-of-state contributions.[39]

The governor's efforts yielded almost nineteen thousand dollars in cash, plus a sizable amount of food and clothing. The bulk came from other counties and from Grangers, but churches and individuals from outside the state also helped. Among the contributors to the fund were an eighty-year-old War of 1812 veteran from New York State who thought it was his "duty and privilege to contribute my mite to help the distressed" and enclosed one dollar; the Ojibway Indians of the White Earth Reservation who sent fifty-six dollars, together with a pipe, to signify that they had always been "the true friends of the white man & that they felt the deepest sorrow for their suffering white brothers"; and an "American in Paris" who sent one hundred francs. Although individual contributions were never large, they usually offered an abundance of good will and at least a bit of practical assistance.[40]

When the legislature finally convened in January 1875, Davis reported on his actions to relieve the suffering, and Sibley provided an accounting of the committee's receipts and disbursements. Sibley noted that over three thousand dollars remained in the fund but would be expended shortly, as county commissioners and individuals continued to ask for help. Both men urgently requested substantial legislative action. "It is the duty of the Legislature to act with prudent liberality in the premises," Davis argued, and he called for an appropriation, without specifying an amount. Sibley took a more emphatic stand. He declared that the emergency "imperatively demanded" an appropriation of at least one hundred thousand dollars, plus no less than half that amount more to furnish seed for spring planting. He estimated that twelve to fifteen hundred farmers were "utterly impoverished, and must be relieved by the State, or they will, from necessity, seek some other homes."[41]

The legislature appropriated only twenty thousand dollars "for the immediate relief of the suffering settlers on the frontier of the state, to be expended in providing for them necessary food and clothing." Ramsey County Senator William Murphy had tried without success to raise the sum to fifty thousand dollars. The discussion on his proposal revealed blatant suspicion of the victims — a suspicion obvious in all of the relevant 1875 legislation. In 1874 the legislators, while not overly enthusiastic about becoming involved in relief matters, had not openly questioned the recipients' integrity. This was not the case in 1875. Typical nineteenth-century language about the chronically poor was adopted to discuss these victims. Senator Joseph H. Clark of Dodge County opposed Murphy's attempt to increase the fund, arguing that "these repeated appropriations for aid were calculated to tempt the people to set down and wait for aid." Reports of able-bodied men in frontier counties who had refused work because they were waiting for state relief had apparently convinced him that the needy "should be taught self-reliance" rather than pampered with free aid. Although the senators as a whole may not have shared Clark's attitude, they did soundly defeat Murphy's proposed increase.[42]

The provisions of the bill further suggest a serious mistrust of the victims. The 1874 relief appropriation had left the disbursement of the money to the governor's discretion. The 1875 bill had the same feature, but it added stipulations that required, in effect, a means test of the recipients. It demanded that each applicant provide a "duly verified" petition "showing the necessity of such relief," signed by a majority of the town supervisors or county commissioners. At the very least these regulations systematized and cemented the less formal distribution system that Davis had instituted in 1874. At worst it cast the recipients into the role of paupers and demanded means tests similar to those required of the chronically poor.[43]

The legislators wrote similar "safeguards," presumably to protect the state's interests and not the victims', into a bill that extended the time for payment of personal property taxes. The 1874 law included no conditions, but the 1875 bill allowed extensions only to those who could "make proof under oath to the satisfaction of the county treasurer" that they were unable to pay their taxes because of crop loss. Unlike the 1874 law, which implicitly included all taxpayers in the afflicted counties, this one offered no relief to those who suffered indirectly from the grasshopper plagues, particularly shopkeepers and merchants. A similar 1875 law exempted frontier settlers from interest or penalties for the nonpayment of real estate taxes if the settler could prove under oath that through the loss of his crops he was "rendered incapable" of paying the taxes. The law further stated: "False swearing under this act shall be construed to be perjury, and subject the party taking such oath to the punishment prescribed for that crime."[44]

In early March the legislature appropriated seventy-five thousand dollars for the purchase of seed grain and allowed up to a third of that for immediate relief, if necessary. Instead of investing the governor with authority to distribute the grain — as the 1874 law had — this measure called on him to appoint, with the advice and consent of the senate, three commissioners to manage and disburse the funds. The legislation did not add specific stipulations for distribution.[45]

Of the twenty thousand dollars appropriated in January 1875 for direct relief, less than half was given out. "It was not found necessary to expend the whole of this sum," Davis reported. But his correspondence tells a different story. In mid-March a Martin County official complained to Davis that "The bill appropriating $20,000 for food & clothing seems to be so closely guarded as to be out of reach to nearly all." He reported further that only one man in the area had so far taken the oath required, and he was "*wholly without means.*" The official could not believe that the governor would uphold standards so rigid that only the completely destitute could apply. Another official asked the governor to clarify the requirements because, as he read them, they demanded that the recipients "can not have anything at all" in order to qualify. Unfortunately for the settlers, this was the case. If a farmer owned a cow or a team he failed to meet the requirements. Some farmers simply refused to take an oath that so clearly and publicly labeled them paupers; they rejected assistance that robbed them of their dignity. A Jackson County commissioner wrote that the Scandinavians in his county would kill their last cow and eat it before they would take the oath. Other farmers declined to damage themselves further by selling their last cow or their only team. Without a cow, a settler would be completely dependent on a not overly generous state government. Without a team, he could not plow in the spring, and he would be unable to help himself. These farmers, therefore, could not take the oath and could not receive help.[46]

County reports cast further doubt on Davis' statement that it was not necessary to use the entire appropriation. The Renville County commissioners received only four hundred dollars of the state funds and found it clearly insufficient, as it allowed only about one dollar to each family that urgently needed both food and clothing. The small allocation caused "suffering to a great extent" for many settlers. In Rock County, too, the amount "fell short of the requirements."[47]

The stricken farmers, unable to get what they needed, took what was offered. In 1875 in Martin County 25 percent of the families applied for and received aid. H. R. Rense, a farmer in Fairmont Township, received the county's largest allotment, including sugar, rice, tea, and medicine worth a total of $10.24. In two more typical cases Hiram Clark and George Anson obtained considerably less. On March 9, 1875, Clark presented himself to the town clerk and swore in the presence of two witnesses to be "wholly without means" with the exception of a yoke of oxen and one cow. The Clark family — husband, pregnant wife, and six children — received only $5.95 worth of flour, sugar, dried apples, and tea, doubtless because he had not sold his oxen and cow. George Anson, who had a wife and four children, proved his destitution and got $1.13 worth of pork and $.52 worth of molasses. These amounts could not have carried the recipients far.[48]

Davis also reported to the legislature that it had been unnecessary to allocate all of the seed-grain appropriation. "It was found that the object of the statute could be effectually accomplished with $50,000" and therefore the seed commissioners received only that amount. Perhaps this decision resulted from a close study of the situation, as Davis suggested, but other sources reveal something different. The *Martin County Sentinel* reported that the visiting seed-wheat commissioners stated that the county's appropriation would be part of a total sum of fifty thousand dollars — not seventy-five thousand dollars. "Owing to the empty condition of the State Treasury," the commissioners could not borrow more than fifty thousand dollars on state credit. A Nobles County historian verified this report, arguing that because of the tight money market the state simply could not procure the extra funds. A promise to negotiate for the additional twenty-five thousand dollars did not materialize. Even the normally optimistic *St. Paul Daily Pioneer* reported that the applications for seed "would exhaust an appropriation of half a million dollars" and that the sum available would not satisfy "more than a meager fraction of the demand." Whatever the governor's arguments to the contrary, most victims agreed that even the whole of the apportionment "fell far short of being sufficient to seed the ground."[49]

The state relief appropriation thoroughly failed to meet the needs, and the allocation of seed provided farmers only the barest minimum. Certainly the depression of the mid-1870s kept assistance at a parsimonious level. Yet, the carefully designed legislation gives a better clue to the lawmakers' motives. The regulations suggest that the legislators questioned the legitimacy of the need and the integrity of the supplicants. The needy appeared not as disaster victims but as paupers — the habitually needy — who called repeatedly on the public for assistance. Their condition did not seem to improve from year to year, nor did they seem able to help themselves. That the victims, through no fault of their own, could not improve their condition did not deter the lawmakers from suspicion, fear, and self-righteousness — the usual attitudes toward the poor.

Neither Sibley nor Davis shared these views about the victims. The two may well have believed with typical Americans that most poverty resulted from personal failing but that such a judgment did not apply in these circumstances. These were people who battled a natural disaster and needed temporary help; above all, they might leave the state and thereby diminish its potential prosperity. The last

81

fact alone constituted sufficient reason to act. The two men kept the plight of the suffering a public issue. They showed serious commitment to supplying assistance. It is doubtful that the legislators would have taken even the action that they did without the active intervention of Davis and, more significantly, Sibley.

In the summer of 1875, when the grasshoppers did only minimal damage, many farmers saved part of their crops. Thus the need for widespread relief abated somewhat and no organized relief efforts took place. In the fall, Davis appointed a three man committee to investigate the habits and characteristics of the grasshoppers. The commissioners personally visited the ravaged areas, sent circulars to town and county officials, and studied the available entomological records. Their goal was to give farmers information to use in protecting themselves against the ravages of the insects. The commission published a fifty-page pamphlet summarizing the basic information, including arrival and departure dates of the grasshoppers, egg laying and hatching patterns, lists of vulnerable crops, and explanations of known methods of destruction.[50]

In the fall Davis chose not to run for re-election. John S. Pillsbury, a former member of Davis' state relief committee, was elected governor. The grasshopper plagues constituted a continuing crisis during the first two years of his administration, but he took a different path from that of Davis.

6

Governor Pillsbury's Response

For many Minnesotans John S. Pillsbury was the right man at the right time. The state suffered from the panic of 1873 and the subsequent depression; the property tax system staggered under high delinquency; an 1874 tax decrease reduced the state's working capital. Minnesotans wanted these problems solved. They wanted no such issues to harass the system again. They were ready to become "modern" Americans, ready for a more efficient, more systematic, more bureaucratized, and more economically accountable government. A majority of the men who voted in 1875 found in Pillsbury the executive they sought: one who shared their frustrations, their hopes, and their interests, and who promised "a businessman's administration of the state government." In January 1876, Pillsbury took office as the eighth governor of Minnesota.[1]

In his inaugural address he laid out his approach to government. "The conditions requisite for the promotion of the public welfare," he declared, "are precisely those essential to success in private affairs." To restore general prosperity, he called for "the practice of a close, methodical and persistent economy"—in both public and private spheres. In the interests of greater frugality and efficiency he called for a smaller legislature and shorter legislative sessions, held biennially rather than annually; consolidation of state offices; employment of a financial examiner and overseer; and a balanced budget.[2]

In his twenty-five-page address Pillsbury called attention to a variety of pressing problems but did not once mention the stricken farmers. While this omission might simply have reflected the reduced damages inflicted by grasshoppers in 1875, it more likely demonstrated Pillsbury's modern and businesslike approach to relief and assistance.

Pillsbury clearly articulated his attitudes in another address issued eight months later. He called earlier state relief efforts "very questionable policy" and warned farmers against relying on such ill-advised public action in the future. Such relief measures, he believed, served as "indemnity for past losses," making up for lost revenue rather than providing food, clothing, and other necessities. Moreover, these practices ran the risk of "weakening the habit of self-reliance" among the recipients. If people received assistance as "indemnity," they would begin to expect it and become a hazard to the well-being of the state and of the individuals themselves. For the good of the state the poor should not expect relief as a right. To protect the poor from their own weak natures, the state should discourage dependence.[3]

In a third address, this one to the legislature in 1877, Pillsbury reiterated his position. "Poverty and deprivation are incidents of frontier life at its best," he stated. Those who experience normal frontier hardships — not legitimately the concern of the state — "are tempted to share the support intended only for the utterly helpless," Pillsbury argued. Although kindness and generosity are intended by the distribution of aid, "the demoralization of a class fully capable of self-support becomes thus inevitable. . . ." He believed that recipients of charity would proceed from taking help not actually needed to "habitual beggary," to "confirmed mendicancy." Through these stages, the farmers' pride and self-respect, "which are the chief stay of an independent people," would become undermined. Well-intended but misdirected state charity would, by causing this decline, be a "deplorable mistake." Therefore, he "felt impelled to firmly discountenance" state relief.[4]

In any case, Pillsbury believed that state aid should be allowed only to those who first proved their willingness to help themselves. Too often state help did not reach those he called "the most worthy recipients," whom he defined as those unwilling to ask for help. In other words, a person who could bring himself to seek aid would lack the moral qualities that made him "worthy" of assistance. Only those who refused to seek public aid were worthy of help, because they had the virtues, the pride, and the integrity to be independent. These people would take aid only if it were pressed upon them. Pillsbury's stand presented for the needy something of an ideological and behavioral trap — though it was not identified as such by the governor.

Pillsbury's attitudes toward the stricken farmers and toward state involvement in their relief were identical to those that had led to the founding of the first Charity Organization Society (COS) in London in 1869 and that accounted for the proliferation of similar organizations throughout the United States, particularly in the Northeast. These groups were proponents of scientific philanthropy, as they called it, and proffered not relief but investigation, advice, and encouragement. Their motto: "Not alms but a friend." Their watchwords: "Kindly but stern."[5]

Pillsbury's statement could have been issued, then, by any of these charitable societies in the United States during the last third of the nineteenth century. He specified what could be considered the "official" — white, middle-class, Anglo-Saxon, Protestant — position toward the needy. He shared the belief that poverty was a disease curable by hard work, virtue, determination, and as little charity as possible. He accepted the principle that relief endangered the giver, the recipient, and the society.

That Pillsbury held such views is not surprising. He was white, middle-class, Anglo-Saxon, and Protestant. Equally important, his own life had demonstrated to him the validity of the American dream. His biography reads something like the Horatio Alger myth, if not the actual stories. He was born in New Hampshire in 1827, to "descendants of early Puritan stock in New England." He had "no special advantages in youth." In 1853 he moved to Minnesota Territory and started a hardware business. The panic of 1857 and a fire that damaged his uninsured store left him with enormous debts. In the face of these difficulties, Pillsbury did not give up, nor did he turn to the government for help. Instead, he borrowed from friends and sought the leniency of his creditors. With their help he rebuilt his operation successfully. In 1873 he joined his nephew Charles in the flour-milling enterprise that, more than a century later, still carries the Pillsbury name. According to one biographer, his became "one of the most distinguished names in the annals of Minneapolis and the commonwealth" and he "occupied a commanding position as one of the leading business men and civic forces in the city."[6]

Pillsbury led an active public life, serving as St. Anthony (later Minneapolis) city councilman, state senator for six terms, and for nearly forty years a University of Minnesota regent. Contemporaries credited him with nearly single-handedly saving the university in the 1860s when it faced financial collapse. He joined and remained for his lifetime a member in good standing of the Congregational church in Minneapolis. Perhaps Pillsbury would have become a member of the New England welfare organizations if he had remained there, so thoroughly did they share attitudes and backgrounds.

When he took office as governor, Minnesota did not face a serious pauperism problem. Yet Pillsbury's understanding of the causes and cures of pauperism profoundly shaped his treatment of the grass-hopper victims. These were farmers, the supposed backbone of the nation, the repositories of the highest American virtues and values. Apparently, when the two "myths" — noble farmer and pauper cul-pable for his poverty — met, the pauper dominated. Pillsbury's fear and condemnation of the pauper were stronger than his respect and admiration for the farmer.

That the farmers became poor through no fault of their own and as a result of conditions obvious even to outsiders made little dif-ference to Pillsbury. Poverty was poverty, and his way of under-standing both the causes and the best methods of relief did not change simply because the actual reason for the poverty changed. Although disaster victims did not fit into the official view, Pillsbury made no distinction between them and paupers.

He was not alone in his identification of the victims as suspect, nor in his attitudes toward poverty and the needy. The *St. Paul Pioneer Press* was, throughout Pillsbury's administration, particularly hostile and censorious toward the settlers. An editorial in 1876 argued that the "better class of people" throughout Minnesota objected to gov-ernment assistance because it had a "very demoralizing effect" and tended to "educate people who from any cause are unfortunate into relying, not on their own exertions, but on state aid to help them out." Another editorial explicitly accused the grasshopper sufferers of lacking the will characteristic of other poor people. "Hundreds of farmers will sit listlessly down and do nothing to destroy the 'hop-pers, relying either upon a State bounty to pay them for catching them, or upon State aid to provide them with subsistence." Cer-tainly, the paper argued, grasshoppers brought disaster, but "no disaster could befall the infested districts so great as to encourage this suicidal indolence or the expectations which foster it." The lazy deserved neither help nor sympathy. "If anybody chooses to lie down and be eaten up by grasshoppers, we don't care much if he is de-voured body, boots, and breeches. If he fights and keeps on fighting, the cases will be rare in which he fails; but if he does fail then he is entitled to sympathy, and only then."[7]

In yet another editorial the *Pioneer Press* stated flatly that most of the relief appropriations offered by the 1874 and 1875 legislatures had been "absorbed by the designing," because the worthy had too much self-respect to "compete for public funds with the clamorous crowds of greedy mendicants, whose lying impudence elbowed aside the modesty of genuine distress and shamed it into self-concealment." Even though recipients of earlier assistance had been required to submit documentary proof of their need, it was, the newspaper stated, "universally" believed that most of the money had been wasted. The St. Paul newspaper went so far as to argue that the "slipshod, good-natured indiscriminate distribution of public bounty" of the previous years had done more public harm than private good. It taught the settlers, "especially those from foreign countries," to become permanent mendicants. It taught them to depend, not on their own efforts for survival, but on the state. The *Pioneer Press*, as evidence for its claims, printed a letter from an unnamed "German farmer" in an unnamed southwestern county to unidentified friends in the old country: "This is a good country, it yields large crops, and if the crops fail the government takes care of you." It was to protect the interests of the state, of the stricken communities, and of the truly needy and to foil the illegitimate efforts of the unworthy that the *Pioneer Press* opposed state action and applauded Pillsbury.[8]

Nor was this view of the grasshopper victims peculiar to Pillsbury and the *Pioneer Press* or new in 1876. In 1874 the *Worthington Western Advance* editorialized that the best assistance would "help men to help themselves." The auditor in Watonwan County — where the grasshoppers ravaged repeatedly — feared for the moral welfare of the people. He stated, "That we have many in the county who are very poor and some actually destitute of the necessaries of life is beyond dispute but could the supplies now sent us have been withheld until winter and the people induced to rely more upon their own exertions for their subsistence it would have been better." He did not explain what "better" meant.[9]

The governor's espousal of such sentiments in 1876 helped to crystallize and focus an attitude that already existed within the state. His stand seemed to fuel the *Pioneer Press* attack. And his beliefs significantly affected the response of the legislature during 1876, 1877, and 1878. He did not once call for state-funded direct assistance to farmers, as Governors Davis and Austin had in previous years.

Instead, in 1876 Pillsbury called on the farmers to help themselves in "timely, concerted and persistent efforts to fight the grasshoppers." He urged those "most directly involved" to meet in their counties to devise collective actions. This proclamation reads like a call to arms — replete with martial language. "I earnestly invoke the united and resolute action of the people in a manful defense against a common enemy. . . . Let the common enemy be thus fought at every stage of his existence and at every point of his attack." To help fight the battle, he described the best-known methods for destroying the pests.[10]

In 1877 the governor submitted to the legislature a long list of proposals to help the farmers but did not include one for direct relief. He outlined a program that included township-, county-, and state-funded bounties, revision of the game laws to protect natural predators of the grasshoppers, appointment of an entomological commission, a reward for the best hopperdozer design, an investigative committee, and authorization for townships to levy a tax for firebreaks and ditches.[11]

Pillsbury's dedication to purging the state of the pests was more than idle talk; he was willing to do his part. In October 1876 in Omaha, Nebraska, Pillsbury convened a meeting of the governors of those western states and territories afflicted by the grasshoppers. His purpose was to "secure combined action in resistance of the growing evil." The governors prepared an extensive list of extermination suggestions and mandated its distribution throughout the ravaged and threatened areas. This kind of assistance to needy farmers was just what Pillsbury had in mind. It helped them, he thought, without demoralizing them, without subjecting them to loss of self-esteem, or without endangering the moral integrity of the state.[12]

Pillsbury assured the settlers that if they answered his call to aid themselves and still failed, they could console themselves that they had "made such helpful and assiduous attempts as deserved success." And, as he told the legislature, those who struggled to hold on to their land in the face of such misfortune and who displayed fortitude and self-reliance deserved the "tenderest consideration."[13]

When the needy demonstrated that they were not and would not become "paupers," when they showed that they would not be corrupted by aid, and when they made clear that they did not want to accept help, then they merited assistance. Then Pillsbury personally would help them. In late December 1876 and again in January 1877, he toured the stricken counties of southwestern Minnesota. Traveling incognito, without publicity or fanfare, he dressed in common clothes and presented himself to individual settlers as an interested and concerned stranger. He "mingl[ed] with the people around their hay fires, witness[ed] their scanty clothing, and [partook] of their humble fare." His goal, he said, was to get a true look, instead of relying on unsubstantiated, exaggerated, and fabricated reports.[14]

The *Pioneer Press* reported on the governor's visits in language that sentimentalized both Pillsbury and the needy and, not coincidentally, rationalized a patronizing attitude toward the sufferers. Pillsbury found "actual want" only in isolated cases. Among the most needy were many of the "better class" who, "unaccustomed to want," tried to hide their privations from "inquisitive strangers," including the governor posing as a stranger. When asked about their deprivations, these proud people, characterized by "manly pride" and "woman[ly] delicacy," described their neighbors' conditions but asked nothing for themselves. Only when the governor revealed his identity and promised that no names would be made public did they tell their own stories. One "typical" man, surrounded by children in ragged clothing, protested that they could "pull through well enough." When the governor urged the farmer to accept aid, at least for his children, "His father's heart exploded through his mask of proud reserve," and his "strong frame convulsed with sobs." He accepted Pillsbury's help. These were the kinds of people that the governor wanted to assist. Relief would not corrupt them and they would not squander what they received. Furthermore, these were the very people who had been excluded from previous relief because the "well-to-do mendicant" capitalized on the state's generosity. These truly needy, those from the "better class" who neither wanted nor asked for government relief, agreed that such appropriations usually went to men "who are not ashamed to practice all the arts of professional mendicancy to divert to their well-filled larders the relief intended for the destitute alone."[15]

Years later, Philip W. Pillsbury, the governor's grandson, recalled a particularly romantic story about how his grandfather, during one of these winter trips, met a settler who had no overcoat and no money to buy one. The governor removed his own coat, gave it to the man, and returned to town coatless.[16]

Pillsbury's experiences among people whom he considered truly needy demonstrated to him "the urgent necessity of immediate action," for which he turned, not to the state government, but to

private citizens. He requested contributions from churches, benevolent associations, and the citizens of Minnesota. The appeal circulated widely and, in late December 1876 and early January 1877,
contributions poured into the state capital. Governor Pillsbury personally supervised the collection and distribution of these donations.
His suspicion that too often the unworthy received what should go
to the industrious and honest poor motivated the most careful investigation of the recipients. And the only way to guarantee that the
"idle and vicious" did not receive unwarranted aid, he believed, was
to require personal inspection by the benefactors and to set strict
limits on eligibility.[17]

E. W. Chase, manager of the St. Paul Society for Improving the
Condition of the Poor, offered suggestions based on his experience.
He recommended employing "judicious advice and encouragement"
to compel the needy farmers to use more diligently the resources they
already possessed. The needy would never learn to help themselves,
he argued, if outsiders persisted in "thoughtless and promiscuous
charity." Public generosity ran the risk of "undermining the spirit of
self-dependence so essential to a pioneer life, and arousing hopes of
future aid in every little emergency." Chase urged as a general rule
that goods — never cash — be given out. Recipients of money, he
believed, would squander it on liquor or other luxuries instead of
spending it on "necessities."[18]

Chase echoed the sentiments of professional charity workers
throughout the country: "Is it not equally true that it is a doubtful
if not a dangerous precedent for the state to assume to equalize the
irregularities of providence or (which is more often the case) of
improvidence, which always has, and always will, occasionally dis-
turb the body politic?" In this passage, Chase showed how easily the
connection could be made between the danger of helping the poor
and that of helping the disaster victims.

In the spirit of the charity organization societies, Pillsbury personally visited the needy; he appealed for aid; he collected contributions; he set the rules for eligibility. The *St. Paul Pioneer Press*
congratulated him for adopting "such a searching system of ante-
cedent investigation as would bring to light every meritorious case of
destitution, and enable him to confine the aid to those cases only."
Pillsbury personally oversaw the allocation of foodstuffs; no money
was distributed, as Chase had advised.[19]

Mahala Fisk Pillsbury, wife of the governor, supervised the allotment of the nonfood contributions. She was an active volunteer charity worker in Minneapolis and no doubt was well informed about the current thinking on charity and relief. She served as the first president of the Minneapolis Children's Home Society. She knew how to handle the poor, assess their needs, judge their characters, and prevent fraud and malingering. In lieu of a Minneapolis charity organization society, Mahala Pillsbury could be counted on to be cautious in giving assistance.[20]

The citizens of Winona, a small town on Minnesota's eastern border, took the governor's appeal seriously but by-passed his distribution system. Participants at a meeting called by several clergymen passed two resolutions. They first argued forcefully that the state had a "duty" to appropriate at once "such a sum of money as may be required to supply the necessaries of life" to the needy in southwestern Minnesota. The state could better afford to assist the sufferers than to force them out by ignoring their needs. The second resolution called on the people of Winona for contributions. That night over two thousand dollars was pledged and within ten days almost three thousand dollars had been collected. The group appointed a committee to appeal to the boards of trade of both Chicago and Milwaukee for "their aid in the relief of a district which contributes so much to their prosperity." In mid-January a citizens' committee, including the mayor, accompanied five carloads of goods to the southwest area and personally supervised distribution. A week later another committee, "with satchels packed, to remain half the winter if they find it necessary," accompanied another shipment of goods funded by Winona.[21]

The Winona meeting and the resolutions adopted had a different tone from that which characterized Pillsbury's actions and the reporting of the *St. Paul Pioneer Press*. Suspicion did not so thoroughly color their response. Instead they considered assistance a right of the needy, as demonstrated by their appeal to the out-of-state boards of trade. Moreover, they opened their own wallets. Their decision to by-pass Pillsbury suggests either that they disagreed with his system of distribution or that, like him, they wanted to keep personal control over the allocation of their funds.

Their decision brought severe criticism from the *St. Paul Pioneer Press*. The paper charged that by acting without sufficient investigation and caution the Winonans merely continued the mistakes of the past and opened the way for the unworthy to receive help, the very thing that the Pillsbury system aimed to prevent. No doubt, the paper maintained, the Winonans were "grieviously imposed upon" by the "greedy and impudent" when they should have assisted the "really needy" — a charge the *Pioneer Press* failed to document.[22]

The paper also criticized Winona's appeal to the Chicago and Milwaukee boards of trade. Sending "begging committees" who presented Minnesota as a "poverty-stricken mendicant before the world" only hurt the state. If Winonans had allowed the governor to take charge of its contributions, there would have been no need to solicit supplementary funds outside the state, since the available money would have been allocated more wisely.[23]

No doubt many Minnesotans shared these harsh attitudes, and others agreed with Pillsbury's "kindly but stern" conviction that they were doing the best for the needy. Others may have felt similarly about the poor, but did not include the disaster victims in that class. A Minneapolis resident, L. W. Jones, criticized Pillsbury's personal appeal for the needy. "I can name a long list of persons in this city with their thousands," Jones wrote, "who cannot be dragooned into giving a part of their surplus to their suffering fellow-citizens." Moreover, Jones believed that people in need because of the plagues were the responsibility of the whole state and a legislative appropriation would fulfill that duty. Private charity, Jones thought, reduced recipients to "the level of common beggars" and mortified and degraded them by placing them "before the people as beggars of old clothing." The state possessed the resources to care for the people and had an obligation to do so.[24]

Pillsbury remained unmoved by people like Jones, but he did act on the suggestions of church members of several denominations. From time to time in 1876 various groups asked the governor to call a day of prayer, but he took no action. In March 1877 individuals, churches, and public groups sent more urgent requests. A few dissenters argued that a work day — when people throughout the state would offer a day's wages for the sufferers — would be more practical, but the spiritual view persuaded the governor to declare April 26 "a day of fasting, humiliation and prayer." He invited prayers for deliverance from the locust scourge and for comfort for the suffering.[25]

Then, in November, when it seemed that the worst of the plague was finally over, Pillsbury issued a Thanksgiving proclamation asking citizens to join in "fervent manifestations of gratitude to

Almighty God for the numberless blessings vouchsafed us." Let all people, the governor continued, show thanks "by a timely remembrance of those who are yet in need." Various clergymen used this opportunity to appeal once more for contributions for the grasshopper victims and asked Pillsbury again to receive and distribute the assistance. He agreed.[26]

To some twentieth-century observers, Pillsbury and other charity workers in the late nineteenth century appear simply cold and heartless. While their attitudes certainly caused the needy pain, embarrassment, and loss of self-esteem — as well as a lack of adequate provisions — the benevolent did not entirely prevent the allocation of assistance. Sometimes, in fact, they did help people. Unfortunately, they usually did it on their own terms, not on the terms of those in need of help.

Although Pillsbury responded unenthusiastically when settlers asked for emergency relief, he wholeheartedly supported the farmers when they began to make widespread use of hopperdozers. By May 1877 a cheap, easily constructed hopperdozer was developed that required only a strip of sheet metal and a small amount of coal tar. The farmers believed that with a little help from the state government — or some other generous party — they could go far to protect themselves against the damaging losses of previous years. Pillsbury offered coal tar and sheet iron to county commissioners, with the understanding that the counties would reimburse the governor at a later date. In some cases, Pillsbury merely made sure that supplies were available where needed; in others he helped the farmers underwrite the cost. He spent over ten thousand dollars for materials and freight, taking some from his own pocket and some from the direct relief fund appropriated by the legislature.[27]

After the plague had finally passed but not after people still needed some assistance, Pillsbury addressed the 1878 legislature, recommending that the state provide seed loans that would "preserv[e] the self respect of the borrower, and insur[e] his providence." Pillsbury also advised that the state assume all the costs of hopperdozers built the previous summer. This measure, he believed, would encourage self-help and reward the farmers' "commendable efforts . . . which aim at self-protection without hope of reward other than that dictated by enlightened policy."[28]

After 1878 Pillsbury had no further problems caused by grasshopper plagues nor any other natural disaster during his administration. His personal response to the needs of the afflicted farmers garnered for him the reputation of being a man of great compassion and kindness. While that appraisal is not inaccurate, it is one based on a specific idea of the nature of poverty. The professional philanthropists and members of the nineteenth-century charity organization societies would have applauded Pillsbury's efforts to administer "kindly but stern" aid, his attempts to preserve the self-esteem of the recipients, and his wish to prevent the unworthy from receiving assistance intended for the truly needy. The settlers who had seen their crops destroyed and who suffered enormous losses might have agreed with the Cottonwood County farmer who called on the state to use a little less science on the grasshopper; "A little [more] on the golden rule would be better."[29]

7

The "Cold Charity" of the State

In matters of state assistance, the Minnesota legislature traditionally followed where the governors led. Horace Austin asked for appropriations for the victims of prairie fires and hailstorms; Davis asked for relief funds and seed-grain money. In both cases the legislature consented in substance and form, if not in amount. When in 1876 John S. Pillsbury chose not to request relief appropriations from the legislature, the legislators did not initiate either direct relief or seed-grain expenditures. Instead they concentrated on bounties and indirect assistance.

The bounty system — paying for the capture of grasshoppers — had great appeal throughout the state. Besides offering some protection against crop losses, bounties provided what many considered to be the ideal form of relief. Instead of simply giving away money, the government could require that the needy work for assistance. This system answered the demands of those skeptical of public charity: it did not undermine the recipients' initiative; it did not encourage idleness or reward loafing; it did not permit the ineligible to defraud the state; and it did not demoralize the beneficiaries. This mixture of self-righteousness and disdain, as well as "concern" for the needy, was a typical formula for mid-nineteenth-century public relief. The system's only drawback, a serious one, was its cost. In 1875 several counties had offered bounties out of their own treasuries but abandoned the practice when it nearly bankrupted them.[1]

In 1876 the representative from Blue Earth County, which had offered bounties the previous summer, introduced a bill in the legislature calling for state funding of bounties. It faced considerable opposition. Some members argued that it would require nearly unlimited funds. Others questioned whether the whole state should pay for a local affliction. A house committee investigating the matter reported in late February that, although the bounty had been an "eminent success" where given a fair trial, "it is inexpedient to offer a bounty . . . at this time." The house concurred.[2]

The legislators shared the enthusiasm for bounties but did not want to spend the money. So, in a joint resolution, the state house and senate called on the Minnesota congressional delegation to use its best efforts to obtain federal financing. This alternative seemed a perfect way to fund a perfect form of relief, but Congress declined. In another action the legislature legalized the county bounties paid in 1875 and cleared the way for them to be offered in the coming summer. Finally, the legislature agreed to reimburse the counties for half the cost of bounties already paid — an unusually generous act, although the counties had hoped that the state would pick up all of the costs.[3]

The 1876 legislature passed several other bills designed to help the sufferers. A second joint resolution requested that the Minnesota representatives in Congress secure passage of an extension of the time limit for proving up on timber-culture claims. In a further resolution the legislature called on people in infested areas to prepare prairie grasses for burning in the spring when fires could cause maximum damage to the fledgling grasshoppers. The state did not provide seed, as in the previous two years, but did allow counties to do so. Nor did the legislature agree — as it had earlier — to delay tax-payment deadlines, but it did cancel penalties for nonpayment of interest on state lands, if the applicant could prove grasshopper damage.[4]

These measures constitute the entire body of legislation passed to assist the grasshopper sufferers. The state offered no money, but simply called on others to help. For some unfathomable reason, however, the 1876 legislature became known as the "Grasshopper Legislature," a testament more to the quantity and acrimony of debate than to the quality of aid.[5]

In 1877 the legislature went right to work to help the grasshopper sufferers. Early in the session the two houses appointed a joint special committee, chaired by Senator Ignatius Donnelly of Dakota County. It was supported by a two hundred dollar appropriation to handle all costs incurred in studying "the relief of the population of those parts of the State afflicted by grasshoppers." After completing its work, the committee was to recommend such legislation as it deemed necessary. On January 5 Donnelly presented the first from a long list of proposals. He asked the committee on retrenchment to draw up a bill restricting county officials' salaries "to a rate not to exceed the average income of the taxpayers in their respective counties," since he believed it "unjust that the officeholders, who live upon the taxes of the people, should fare better than the people themselves." This bill failed. Another measure proposed limiting the legislative session to a frugal thirty days in order to release encumbered state funds and make the money available for direct aid for the grasshopper sufferers. The legislature killed this bill, too.[6]

In mid-January the legislature ignored Pillsbury's anxiety about the hazards of government relief and responded to the increased losses by unanimously appropriating five thousand dollars for direct relief. It consigned the funds to the governor for distribution "in such manner as he shall deem best fitted to accomplish the purpose hereby intended." The legislature also passed two bills asking the federal government to fund bounties for the destruction of grasshoppers.[7]

Like earlier legislators, the 1877 representatives agreed to abate penalties for nonpayment of interest on the purchase of state lands and to cancel penalties and interest on state taxes. The latter law set strict guidelines: the applicant had to present an affidavit under oath, describing the property, its assessed value, and the tax levied. He then was to swear that he could not pay the taxes due before December 1, 1877, because of his loss from grasshopper damage. Furthermore, each applicant had to supply two "disinterested residents of such county" to substantiate his claim that he had lost crops and for that reason – and not other causes – could not pay the taxes levied. The affidavits and the witnesses' certificates were to be filed with the county auditor, who was told in the legislation the exact wording to be used to note the abatement on the tax list. Again, it is clear that the legislature was attempting to prohibit all but the most needy from taking advantage of the law.[8]

Another 1877 law required that each grasshopper-infested county appoint someone to superintend the burning of prairie grass and to prevent burning before May 15 "in each and every year." The legislators hoped that the grasshoppers were a temporary affliction, but in case the plague proved to be a permanent condition, the counties would be partially protected by the control of prairie fires. In other attempts to subdue the pests, the legislators called on county governments in afflicted areas to hire at least one hopperdozer to destroy the insects. Compensation would be paid out of the local treasury. Finally, the legislators assessed every male inhabitant in the infested area, excepting only paupers, idiots, lunatics, and those over sixty or under twenty-one, one day of work per week for five weeks to assist in eliminating the grasshoppers. A man could buy his way out of this service by paying the town bounty fund one dollar for each day assessed and by finding "some suitable and efficient person" to replace him and pay him a wage of one dollar per day. Anyone who neglected this responsibility could be fined ten dollars or sentenced to ten days in jail. It is unclear whether these laws were enforced. None of them aroused much opposition, because they did not require state expenditures.[9]

Two pieces of grasshopper legislation, however, demanded large appropriations: the seed-grain and bounty laws, both of which provoked considerable controversy. Legislation introduced in the 1877 session made available seventy-five thousand dollars for loans to purchase seed grain for farmers. As adopted into law, the measure established even more elaborate bureaucratic procedures than for earlier seed grants. First, the law mandated how the loans would be publicized: each town clerk was to post notices in the three most prominent places in the township. Second, all applicants were required to provide sworn statements "showing the condition of their property, both real and personal, and whether incumbered by mortgage or otherwise." Then in the presence of a justice of the peace or other official, each applicant had to swear that "he or she is utterly unable, by any resource of their own to procure seed grain. . . ." The law also required that at least two witnesses swear to the validity of the applicant's claim. The declaration, the affidavit, and the witnesses' statement were to be filed with the county auditor and be open to public inspection. Any person found guilty of swearing falsely was liable for perjury. The county commissioners and auditor were instructed to determine the "worthy" applicants and to forward a certified list of their names to the governor.[10]

The law made further stipulations. The governor was to give each county a proportionate share of the appropriation, and each qualified applicant would receive an equal part. County officials would then handle the actual distribution of the seed, not the money. The legislators, still not assured that they had covered every possibility of fraud, instructed county commissioners to require a promise from each recipient not to sell the seed. All of these precautions were written into a law that allowed a maximum of twenty-five dollars worth of seed per person.

The 1877 seed appropriation differed from earlier ones in its greater detail and its requirement of added applicant information, but the most significant variation was that it offered loans — not gifts — of seed. During the two years following assignment of the seed, the recipients were to be taxed for its entire value. The loan carried no interest, but it did constitute a first lien on crops raised in that period. If the grasshoppers took another crop and the farmers offered proof of their losses, the repayment period would be extended for another year without penalty or interest. If recipients defaulted on their loans, the responsibility for repayment would fall to the whole county and would be met by a special county-wide tax.

The law reflected more fear of fraud than active sympathy for the sufferers, and it excluded all but the most desperate. Its stringent requirements eliminated many; others would exclude themselves because of the built-in potential for humiliation. And, indeed, it removed the sufferers whom Governor Pillsbury most wanted to assist — those who helped themselves. Requiring the recipient to be "utterly unable" to procure seed without help effectively shut out anyone who had been able to save a cow or two, or a team, and who could not, therefore, be considered wholly without means. When the Martin County commissioners sent the governor their list of "approved" applicants, they appended this note: "We believe that there is ten times as much needed but the oath is such that it is believed that a man can own nothing & take said oath." Despite the severe requirements, county authorities forwarded almost three thousand applications within a month after the passage of the law. In all, almost four thousand farmers proved their eligibility. With so many qualified applicants, the appropriation did not stretch far enough to provide each with the maximum of even twenty-five dollars worth of seed. Instead, each received about twenty-one dollars worth. If the recipients took their entire allotment in wheat seed, each would be able to plant about thirteen acres. At a yield of sixteen bushels to the acre — the average for the state in 1877 — a farmer would stand to gross about two hundred dollars. Thus the limited aid would at best result in limited recovery.[11]

The law faced a variety of criticisms. A Windom farmer grumbled that the money was "as good as thrown away," for wheat and grasshoppers could not grow on the same land, and the grasshoppers already had first claim. Others complained that the allotment could not satisfy even minimal needs. One citizen decried the "cold charity" of the state, and argued that Shylock himself could not have devised "more rending terms." A Stevens County farmer, "one of the hopper-dozed" as he described himself, voiced the harshest criticism. The legislature, he said, made a "great mistake in limiting the farmer to a less quantity of seed than would sow all the land he had prepared for seed." If more had been allowed, he argued, the farmers could have repaid their debts at harvesttime and the entire community would have benefited. Since the money was not a gift but a loan, the state could certainly have offered more. "The appropriation of the pitiful sum of seventy-five thousand dollars," he concluded, "is making a promise to the ear and breaking it to the heart, and [it] is not worthy of the great state of Minnesota to do such a small thing."[12]

The *Pioneer Press* defended the bill and the legislature against this attack in an editorial that ran to almost two thousand words. The writer carefully and patiently (but condescendingly) explained to the Stevens County farmer, and all others who shared this "odd" opinion about the role of the state government, that the appropriation was "intended as a method of temporary relief for cases of extreme poverty." The plan was not to give farmers enough to pay their debts, only sufficient to eat; so it offered a "charity loan" rather than a business loan. The legislature had not made a great mistake; it had averted an even greater error. If the state gave business loans, any farmer, mechanic, or other citizen who got into debt would have an equal claim on this bounty. Loans of this kind would bankrupt the state; and, more importantly, it would "bankrupt all the moral resources of the State; it would sap and destroy those vital energies of self-reliance and self-helpfulness on which the physical and social progress and prosperity of a people depend."[13]

Most significantly, the *Pioneer Press* editorialized, "No greater calamity can befall a people than to educate them in the belief that it is the duty of the government to take care of their private interests; than to teach them to rely not on their own exertions, their own prudence, their own energies for the means of self-support or of overcoming the difficulties with which all have to struggle in acquiring the means of subsistence or physical comfort; but to depend on the government." This kind of servile dependence had no place in a free country, the *Pioneer Press* argued; the goal of free government was to enable people to be independent and ensure that they reaped the rewards of their own industry and thrift. To do otherwise, to encourage citizens inequally, would "destroy all the incentives to self-reliance which lie at the bottom of the whole scheme of civil liberty. . . ." When the moral and financial rectitude of the state, as well as the very way of life of a free people were at stake, the legislature could not do otherwise than to tread carefully. The editorial's extended rationale, if shared by citizens and their elected representatives, goes far to explain the appropriation and its stringent provisions.

The 1877 legislature, in further action, passed a bounty law that provoked even greater controversy. The session should have been labeled the "Bounty Legislature," since its members spent so much time on the bill. Moreover, for the two months following its passage, no other single issue (or combination of issues) so dominated the governor's attention. The law allocated one hundred thousand dollars "to provide for the destruction of grasshoppers and their eggs." It promoted self-help and provided an indirect form of relief that did not demean the recipients. The legislation set a sliding scale of payments, pegged to dates that roughly coincided with the developmental stages of the insects — from one dollar per bushel before May 25 to twenty cents per bushel after July 1. This arrangement encouraged collection during periods when the insects posed the greatest threat. The law required the governor to appoint a "competent person" in each township to receive, measure, and destroy the insects gathered, to be compensated from county funds with "such sums as the county commissioners may determine." If more grasshoppers were caught than could be paid for out of the appropriation, the claims would be prorated at the state level and the balance paid by the counties.[14]

The measure had a variety of critics, but none so strident as the *Pioneer Press*. The newspaper launched its first attack immediately following the bill's introduction. Believing the bounty essential to "lift the dead weight of impotent despair" from the shoulders of the afflicted farmers, the *Pioneer Press* nonetheless objected that by providing state funding the law supplied no incentive for "vigilant watchfulness" in the counties against the "improvident or dishonest application of the bounties." Only if the county shared some of the financial burden would the officials be careful and frugal. Senator William H. Folsom of Chisago County (an area free of the insects) agreed and tried to reduce the appropriation by 60 percent and to force the counties to allocate an equal amount. Minneapolis Senator

Levi Butler, a lumberman, arguing that the state should help only those who helped themselves, supported the change. He "doubted the propriety of encouraging the people to rely entirely upon the State for assistance." Senator S. A. Hill, a Yellow Medicine County farmer, opposed the amendment, protesting that the bill would benefit the entire state by halting the eastward march of the pests. And the Sibley County senator argued that the most seriously infested counties had suffered repeated losses and could least afford such an expenditure. To pass the amendment would effectively defeat the intent of the bill. The amendment failed.[15]

The *Pioneer Press* launched another attack, suggesting an alternative title for the bill: "An act to organize a raid on the State Treasury and encourage the production of grasshoppers." It harshly criticized the legislators who opposed the reduction in state funding: "The men haunted with the ghosts of murdered political prospects seemed to speak in bated breath and vied with each other in what they termed 'relieving the sufferers.'" The *Pioneer Press* could find no "honest excuse" for the passage of such an ill-considered law. Ill-considered or not, the bill became law on March 1, 1877, when Pillsbury reluctantly affixed his signature.[16]

The controversy continued relentlessly. In March and April the locusts began to hatch, but the governor made no move to appoint measurers. During those two months Pillsbury received no fewer than one hundred nominations — some by individuals (usually themselves), some offered by private groups, some by county officials. The nominating letters in March read as simple requests for the appointment of specific persons. In April the letters sounded more frantic; the hoppers were hatching and action had to be taken soon. By the middle of May nominations gave way to frenzied pleas that someone, anyone, be appointed.[17]

But many people, fearing the possible effects of implementing the law, had also written to Pillsbury asking him not to make the appointments, thereby effectively preventing any payments. They pointed out that even if the counties paid no bounties above the appropriation, an unlikely possibility, they would have to pay the measurers' salaries, a major expense by itself. The Faribault County commissioners explained that they would need twenty measurers. At a fair wage of two dollars per day the county would have to pay forty dollars per day for up to six months — an amount that would impoverish the people more than the grasshoppers had. Furthermore,

102

the number of insects was so great that the state fund could not possibly cover the bounties, and the counties would be liable for huge sums. In a second letter a month later, the commissioners estimated that the county might have to pay up to one hundred thousand dollars while it would receive at most four thousand dollars from the state. Various individuals wrote about their fear of the indebtedness the bounty system would cause. Nicollet County citizens pleaded that no appointments be made; members of two Granges argued that enforcement would mean the "virtual confiscation" of their property. Almost one hundred Martin County people asked the governor to ignore the law. As the county auditor noted, "We will have all we can do to weather [the year] without any further debt on ac. of locusts."[18]

The question divided some counties. Petitions and counterpetitions circulated throughout Meeker County in the late spring. The county commission's chairman wrote that "energetic citizens" opposed the appointment, and he implied that the less industrious would exploit the bounties. In Kandiyohi County the disagreements generated at least more paper, if not more heat. About three hundred citizens met in late May to urge the hiring of measurers. The hopelessness of greatly diminishing the grasshopper threat left the farmers disheartened, they argued, and only a bounty system could lift the despair. One correspondent wrote that he had at first opposed the bounty, but that only a person with a "heart of stone" could continue doing so after hearing "the cry of despair, the cry for bread" voiced at the meeting. Moreover, he argued, the governor had sworn to uphold the laws of the state; the bounty plan was now law. The chairman of the county commissioners was not moved. He called the leaders of the meeting self-serving office seekers who showed false sympathy to gain politic ends. He asked the governor to postpone any decision until the petitions arrived. Another Kandiyohi County citizen echoed these sentiments in a "confidential" letter to the governor and argued that only "*political aspirants* and parties of no responsibility" could so mistake the best interests of the county.[19]

Pillsbury might have prevented this ill-will and controversy if he had clarified his position earlier. His inactivity heightened the farmers' fears. Not until late May did he take a public stand against appointing measurers. Convinced that enforcement of the law "would entail upon counties already impoverished by insect ravages a burden of debt which would prove more disasterous than the scourge it was intended to avert," he rejected the requests to act, and the law became a dead letter.[20]

As the next session of the legislature opened in January 1878, an intense feeling of relief pervaded the house and senate chambers. The grasshoppers had gone, and the legislators needed only to help the farmers one last time to get on their feet. For this purpose they appointed a frontier relief committee. The legislators did not memorialize Congress to take any action, nor did they appropriate any direct relief. Instead they postponed payment of taxes for yet another year and approved a seed loan.

The tax law was less stringent than that of 1877, but the seed bill was not. Presumably this appropriation would be the last, but the legislators remained suspicious of the recipients. The 1878 seed-loan law required the applicant to file a statement of real and personal property, as had the 1877 law, and it also required additional information on how many acres the applicant had already prepared for planting, what kind and amount of seed was needed, how many bushels (if any) had been harvested in 1877, how much seed was desired, plus a statement that the applicant needed seed because of grasshopper losses, had no other means of securing it, and wanted it only to plant, not to sell. The papers were again to be filed in the county auditor's office and open to public inspection. After the commissioners evaluated the applicants' eligibility, the governor would apportion the seed. The law stipulated fines or jail sentences for fraudulent use of the seed.[21]

Once again, the appropriation failed to satisfy the needs even of those who qualified under the stringent requirements. In Watonwan County, 132 individuals applied for a total of almost five thousand bushels of wheat and thirteen hundred bushels of oats. The county supplied about 40 percent of the wheat and 65 percent of the oats. All farmers received differing amounts of seed, in contrast to the practice of previous years. The allocation varied according to the number of acres prepared for planting. One farmer was allotted only $5.25 worth of seed; another, $70.00 worth; on the average a Watonwan County applicant got about $19.00 in seed. The total amount allowed varied greatly from county to county. In Martin County, 101 applicants were given an average of $13.00 worth of seed, while in Redwood County 83 applicants received an average of

$29.00 each. It was years before many of these small loans were repaid. Of the 295 farmers who took out loans in Chippewa County, 53 repaid half; another 18 made no payments. As late as 1890, 26 percent of the amount was still outstanding. After ten years, 29 percent of the 1877 loans and 24 percent of the 1878 loans remained unpaid, constituting a total indebtedness to the state of almost sixty thousand dollars. Although counties were held responsible for unsatisfied debts resulting from the 1877 and 1878 seed loans, there is no evidence that the state ever collected.[22]

Neither the legislature nor the governor took further steps to help the farmers. A series of more beneficent years followed the bad ones of 1873–77, and for the next ten years most farmers fared better. The grasshoppers left without laying eggs. Minor infestations of chinch bugs and some particularly dry years caused crop losses in the early 1880s, but did not compel the state to step in again.

In the 1870s both individuals and the state government helped thousands of farmers through bad times. Usually the assistance did not go far enough in relieving the sufferers, but the actions of the legislators were not simply those of unsympathetic fiscal conservatives. The compassion and generosity of many Minnesotans, including the legislators, were confined by a set of attitudes about the poor and about the causes of poverty. Firmly convinced that the needy were responsible for their condition because of idleness, intemperance, or moral laxity, the benevolent believed that indiscriminate charity merely deepened dependence. Thus to offer aid willy-nilly and without sufficient safeguards both for the state and for the recipients damaged both in some way: the state by making itself responsible for continued support and the poor by the undermining of their initiative and self-respect. The generous, therefore, gave charity only to those who could demonstrate their immunity to such undermining effects.

These ideas did not suddenly materialize in 1876 but did sharpen and become a stronger part of the legislation in 1876–78 than in 1873–75. No doubt a number of causes accounted for the apparent shift in legislative attitudes. One reason might well have been that the plagues had continued unabated, and needy settlers persisted in calling for assistance. The legislature, perhaps weary of these endless demands, tightened rather than loosened the state's purse strings. At least as important to the altered attitude of the legislators was the change in the governorship after 1876. Under Governor Cushman K.

Davis relief legislation showed some suspicion of the recipients, but the fears remained diffuse and unfocused. This was true as well of Davis' public position. Unfortunately for the grasshopper sufferers, Davis did not run again in 1876, and John S. Pillsbury replaced him. Pillsbury's views of the relief business differed from Davis'. Relief legislation passed during his administration reflected both his attitudes and his leadership.

8

The Federal Government's Role

The question of federal responsibility for the poor received only intermittent consideration in the late nineteenth century. Section Nine of the United States Constitution gives Congress the power to provide for the "general Welfare of the United States," with the corollary right to make all laws "which shall be Necessary and proper for carrying into Execution the foregoing Powers." Even to the most liberal reformers this clause did not mean that the federal government should take an active part in the care of the indigent.[1]

The federal government itself defined welfare both more generally and more specifically than simply a concern for the indigent. Welfare included care, in the form of pensions and bounties, of soldiers and their families; in 1790, for example, Congress appropriated funds for pensions for disabled veterans of the American Revolution. Welfare included the use of public lands to support schools (the Northwest Ordinance), to provide farms for settlers (the Homestead Act), and to underwrite the costs of higher education (the Morrill Act), as well as to assist in the construction of railroads and public buildings. Welfare also involved incarceration of federal offenders, care of American Indians, and provisions for lepers. In two cases, the federal government broadened its realm of responsibilities: in 1819 and 1826 when Congress donated public lands to the Connecticut and Kentucky asylums for teaching the deaf and dumb.[2]

During the first half of the nineteenth century, however, more than a dozen similar institutions turned to the federal government for support and met with failure. When Dorothea L. Dix requested aid for the mentally ill, Congress in 1854 appropriated ten million acres of public land to support the insane and the deaf and dumb. President Franklin Pierce vetoed the measure, calling the 1819 and 1826 appropriations "mistakes" and vowing not to replicate the error.

Pierce thus narrowed the area of federal responsibility and reinforced the principle of local and private obligation for the needy. "I readily and, I trust, feelingly acknowledge the duty incumbent on us all men and citizens, and as among the highest and holiest of our duties, to provide for those who, in the mysterious order of Providence, are subject to want and to disuse of body or mind"; he wrote, but, "I can not find any authority in the Constitution for making the Federal Government the great almoner of public charity throughout the United States." If the government were to care for the impoverished insane, he argued, it must care for all the indigent. This, he believed, the federal government had no duty to do and, in fact, to assume it would be "contrary to the letter and spirit of the Constitution, and subversive of the whole theory upon which the union of these states is founded." Seeing the precedent already set by the allocations to the Connecticut and Kentucky schools, Pierce wanted to stop such involvement.[3]

President Andrew Johnson's veto of the Freedmen's Bureau bill more than ten years later demonstrates that Pierce's definition of federal responsibility still prevailed. "A system for the support of indigent persons in the United States was never contemplated by the authors of the Constitution," Johnson argued, "nor can any good reason be advanced why, as a permanent establishment, it should be founded for one class or color of our people more than another." The attitudes of such men governed the limits of federal liability until into the twentieth century.[4]

The national government, however, acted consistently during the nineteenth century to relieve victims of natural disaster. Ten times Congress aided suffering people outside the borders of the United States. Two instances involved expenditure of federal money: in 1812 Congress granted fifty thousand dollars for earthquake victims in Venezuela, and in 1897 it allocated fifty thousand dollars for destitute American citizens in Cuba. In other cases Congress authorized the navy to transport provisions — funded by private subscription — to impoverished people in Ireland, France, Germany, India, and Cuba. Of these ten relief measures, six occurred in the years 1897–99. This clustering no doubt represented the increasing strength of the navy and the emergence of the United States as a world power. In the first quarter of the twentieth century, Congress passed more international relief legislation than during the whole of the nineteenth.[5]

The federal government also assisted natural disaster victims at home. From 1803 to 1897 Congress passed thirty relief measures and appropriated over $2 million for these victims. Of the thirty measures, twenty-three were enacted during the last quarter of the century. Moreover, the form of relief changed over the century. In 1803 an extension of time was granted within which to discharge bonds sold to provide aid to fire victims in Portsmouth, New Hampshire. In 1866 contributions to victims of a Portland, Maine, fire were imported free of duty. In 1890 twenty-five thousand dollars was appropriated for tents for flood sufferers and two hundred thousand dollars for starving people in the mining regions of Alaska. These efforts demonstrate an increased federal responsibility for at least one kind of needy.

In the tradition of local and private responsibility, Governor Davis and the Minnesota legislators did not call on the national government for direct involvement in the relief effort for the victims of the grasshopper plague. Because of the precedent of federal involvement in natural disaster relief, however, state officials did request indirect assistance. They asked for aid that could be extended without obligating Congress to appropriate money.

Many stricken farmers looked for work away from home. Usually unable to find employment in their immediate areas, they sought it in other parts of the state. But homesteaders feared that they would lose their rights to the land — either to claim jumpers or by reversion to the government for failure to fulfill the residency requirements. Or they would take work but have to leave their families alone to satisfy homestead regulations. Many farmers found both options unsatisfactory. So, in 1874 legislators called on the federal government to exempt the grasshopper sufferers from the residency requirements.[6]

In June, Senator William Windom of Winona introduced such a measure. "The only object of this bill," he stated, "is to enable the people who have had everything destroyed to leave their preemptions or homestead until the 1st of May, 1875, in order to make a living, in order to support their families; and it provides that the absence shall not operate against their claims." Congress promptly passed the bill; President Ulysses S. Grant signed it; and on June 16, 1874, it became law. In December 1874 Congress extended the provisions of the law, geographically and temporally, to include all homesteaders or pre-emptors on the public lands "whose crops were destroyed or seriously injured by grasshoppers." To those afflicted in 1874 or 1875 "where such grasshoppers shall re-appear," it granted settlers the right to be absent from their lands until July 1, 1876. Twice in 1876, once in 1877, and once in 1878, Congress again extended the exemptions.[7]

State and federal legislators emphasized this form of relief. They paid more attention to it than did the farmers involved. Between 1874 and 1878 just over one hundred settlers made official application for extensions. Either the farmers decided to abandon their lands, or they resisted some of the provisions of the law and chose not to take advantage of it, or they simply did not bother to file.[8]

Three years later, in January 1877 while the Congress contemplated one of the many extensions, a "Hopperdozed Homesteader" voiced his objections. "All the laws heretofore passed on this subject," he wrote, "have proved a positive injury to those who have sought to take advantage of them and have inflicted hardship and suffering on their families." If the settlers had not been allowed to leave, he argued, they would have held on as long as they could, and then abandoned their claims or sold out, leaving the grasshopper country for good. This would have been better, "Hopperdozed" argued, than what did happen. "Families dragged back and forth at all seasons of the year, poorly clothed, living as cheaply as possible, thinking only of saving means to put out a crop." And for what? he asked. To be beaten again and again by the voracious insects, and in the long run to be forced out anyway?[9]

"Hopperdozed" had another objection — no less bitter but more practical. The extensions stipulated that farmers return to their land by July 1 of each year. This provision proved the ignorance of lawmakers, "who don't know anything about how common folks live and get along." If they had specified January 1, farmers could have gone elsewhere to farm for a year, but a midsummer date prohibited the law-abiding from planting and harvesting elsewhere and forced them to return to their own lands in time to see the grasshoppers finish the remains of the crops. Certainly, "Hopperdozed" mused, the legislators, if they had wanted, could have thought of something more practical.

Apparently, however, Congress had the very intention that this disgruntled writer alleged — to keep people on the land. What better way to strengthen the tie than by offering a longer rope? Three other forms of federal assistance had the effect and, no doubt, the goal of encouraging people to reinvest their energy and resources in the farms.

In 1876 Congress amended the Timber Culture Act of 1874 to allow farmers who had planted trees, but lost them to grasshoppers, an extra year for each infestation to prove up their claims without losing their rights. Again in 1878 Congress extended the time. Commissioner S. S. Burdett of the General Land Office also helped by allowing settlers within the stricken region to file final land claims before the county clerk of courts, instead of making the often expensive and inconvenient journey to the nearest land office.[10]

So far, federal involvement consisted of nonfinancial help. In January 1875, however, the government loosened its purse strings and appropriated thirty thousand dollars "to enable the Commissioner of Agriculture to make a special distribution of seeds to the portions of the country which have suffered from grasshopper-ravages during the past summer." The commissioner ordered that the fund be spent on wheat — the farmers' normal cash crop. He instructed Governor Davis to purchase two thousand dollars worth of wheat seed to distribute in "your *own State*" for spring planting. Minnesota's Congressmen Mark L. Dunnell and Horace B. Strait of Shakopee argued that other seeds — buckwheat, turnips, and early corn, beans, and potatoes — would better serve the needs of the farmers by providing them more quickly with food. They could not persuade the commissioner or Governor Davis, who a month later regretted his refusal. His office distributed two thousand bushels of wheat, plus only thirty-one bushels of other seeds. State officials did not distribute the only seed that came to Minnesota from the commissioner of agriculture. With no formality other than a newspaper notice, Congressman Dunnell urged all stricken farmers who lacked seed to write directly to the commission in Washington, "stating the cause of their destitution." By one account, "many hundreds" received seed in this way. Others obtained seed through their Congressmen or through local relief committees.[11]

No doubt many Congressmen congratulated themselves on their generosity. And indeed, as a lump sum thirty thousand dollars seemed a large amount. Divided among grasshopper sufferers in Kansas, Nebraska, Iowa, Dakota Territory, as well as Minnesota, however, such a total did not plant many rows for any one farmer. Settlers could not even feed their families, let alone exploit the government's generosity with such amounts. Of course it was better than nothing, and Congress was not in the habit of granting seed to farmers.

In 1877 Senator P. W. Hitchcock of Nebraska asked for another appropriation of thirty thousand dollars. Senator Ingalls from Kansas called this amount "a very small contribution that Congress can make to furnish them [the sufferers] with the means of seeding their ground anew." But West Virginia Senator Henry Davis called it "extravagant" and argued, "I see no reason why a particular section of the country should be singled out and favored." After some haggling, the Senate pared the allocation to twenty-five thousand dollars. The *Glencoe Register* suggested that without the federal grant many farmers would have given up their fight against the grasshoppers. And, it stated with a hint of sarcasm, the seed went to a good purpose — that of feeding the pests. Farmers could not afford to use their own seed for that purpose.[12]

Congressman Strait, having already drunk twice from the well of federal benevolence, tried again in 1878 to get the commissioner of agriculture — now William G. Le Duc, a Minnesota resident — to make a special distribution of seed. Unfortunately Le Duc replied that he could take no definite action. Congress had not approved a special appropriation, and the department could not provide extra seed for a particular group. "Nothing seems to remain now," he wrote, "but that they should come under the general distribution provided by law for all sections of the Union."[13]

These measures constituted the bulk of federal involvement in the relief of the victims that followed the tradition of federal responses to disaster. Each action aimed to keep the farmers on their land. In some cases, farmers and legislators disagreed about the efficacy of the measures. In other instances, on-the-scene witnesses objected to the manner of assistance. At any rate, each grant provided only a minimum of aid.

———

These efforts might have constituted the entirety of federal involvement but for the active advocacy of one man, Brigadier General E. O. C. Ord, commanding officer of the United States Army Department of the Platte in Omaha, Nebraska. Other individuals and groups had tried to get federal assistance, but they met with little success. Sidney Dillon of North Platte, Nebraska, for example, telegraphed Secretary of War William Belknap in late 1874 asking if the Union Pacific Railroad could purchase government clothing "at very low prices" to be distributed to grasshopper sufferers. The secretary replied that all "old pattern" clothing must, according to law, be sold at public auction after due notice. New pattern clothing on hand had to be issued to the troops. Therefore, the army had no authority to make such a sale, Belknap informed Dillon.[14]

In late 1874 the Cincinnati Chamber of Commerce recommended to Belknap that clothing stored at the nearby Jeffersonville, Indiana, supply depot be donated to the destitute of Nebraska. The adjutant general, after investigating the military stores at the depot, reported on the supplies of blankets and clothing, but nothing came of the Cincinnati request. In July 1875, just one month before his death, Charles Grandison Finney, prominent antebellum revivalist then in residence at Oberlin College, wrote directly to President Grant asking for federal assistance for the grasshopper sufferers. Finney did not even merit a response.[15]

General Ord met with more success, although not without persistent effort. Compelled by state resistance to aiding the sufferers, a private group organized the Nebraska Relief and Aid Association to collect and distribute food, money, clothing, fuel, and seed to citizens "reduced to necessitous circumstances." The association named Nebraska Governor Robert W. Furnas chairman. He had, however, been skeptical about the validity of reports on destitution and had rejected requests for state assistance. Thus, he functioned as a figurehead who added official sanction to the association's cause. The committee chose General Ord as vice-chairman, and most responsibility fell to him. As headquarters, the group selected Omaha, Ord's post of duty. If in choosing Ord the committee hoped to gain access to federal resources for the relief effort, they made a wise decision.[16]

During his involvement with the Nebraska association, Ord consistently drew on his authority as commanding general of the Department of the Platte. In late fall he ordered Major James S. Brisbin to tour some of the most stricken counties in southwestern Nebraska because "the aid societies cannot reach the most destitute cases." Brisbin found farm families near starvation and without money, credit, or even ammunition for hunting. Moved by this report and by other information and compelled by the inadequacy of private efforts and the state's refusal to help, Ord turned to the federal government. In late October 1874 he requested authority "to send, by reliable officers, to each of four of the most stricken counties two or three thousand rations of bread or flour and pork," to be distributed "to those in danger of starvation." On the same day, Ord sent Major N. A. M. Dudley to five other Nebraska counties and, without official permission, ordered him to distribute small supplies of emergency food. Dudley was most moved by a family of four that had only ten pounds of flour, from the relief committee, and two pounds of pork, from a more well-to-do neighbor. In language that would have fit comfortably in the report of a Philadelphia friendly visitor, Dudley reported that the man, "with quivering lips and moistened eye," said he did not know how he could get more supplies. Dudley, seeing this scene again and again in various forms, concluded that "Great suffering" existed throughout the region. He predicted that without sufficient provisions for the winter, hundreds would starve.[17]

Commissary-General of Subsistence A. E. Shiras, in the meantime, reported that the army subsistence appropriation for the year was so far depleted that "it will be impracticable for the Subsistence Department to afford any relief to the destitute inhabitants of Nebraska." The secretary of war concurred, and on November 7 Shiras denied Ord's request.

Dissatisfied with the response, Ord a few days later telegraphed copies of Brisbin's and Dudley's reports to the War Department. His covering letter reiterated the request strongly. The two reports, he said, "show that unless relieved soon many poor frontier people will certainly starve to death, while the Army store-houses within 100 miles are filled with provisions." He realized that the law prohibited the issue of military stores for such cases, but he strongly believed that Congress would willingly approve – retroactively – "any issue of supplies necessary to save lives of our own people." While not quite threatening to go over the heads of army officials to make his case to Congress, he certainly implied that federal legislators would look with strong disfavor on the army's willingness to let people starve.

Again Ord's efforts netted only negative results. Comfortably situated in Chicago, Lieutenant General Philip H. Sheridan, commander of the Military Division of the Missouri, objected. "It is a little unwise," Sheridan wrote, "to compromise the Government by the action of its military officers in regard to any general distribution of supplies." Voicing a lack of compassion and an abundance of suspicion not unusual among those unacquainted with the actual conditions, Sheridan continued, "There may be a good deal of suffering in portions of Nebraska, but if the Government takes any advanced steps to relieve it, the suffering will be magnified a hundred times more than it really is." While approving of the distribution already made by Dudley, Sheridan recommended "a good deal of caution" in future dispensing of military supplies, his polite way of suggesting that goods not be issued. Fortunately for the frontier settlers, Sheridan's position was not entirely shared by the secretary of war, who authorized the issue of military clothing in Kansas and Nebraska but refused to allow distribution of army food.[18]

Throughout the months Ord worked to secure federal authorization to supply food and additional clothing, individual farmers wrote to President Grant imploring him to offer help. Usually Grant forwarded these appeals to the secretary of war, who routinely filed them without reply. In one case, however, Belknap approved a petition from stricken citizens. The people of Rush and Paines counties in Kansas asked that the wood contract at nearby Fort Larned be increased by five hundred cords. If citizens could be hired to provide the wood, they could survive without asking for government aid. The quartermaster general reported that "no loss to the U.S." would result from acquiring the additional wood. The secretary authorized the purchase, provided it accomplished its stated goal and "the petition is not designed to favor certain contractors but is in truth designed for the relief of the suffering citizens."[19]

The suspicions of Belknap and Sheridan, as well as the former's refusal to authorize food distribution, may be attributed to their strong dedication to the law and possibly to military discipline. They may also show the vitality of nineteenth-century attitudes about the responsibility of the federal government and about those who needed aid. The reports of conditions, verified by a commanding general, supported by numerous reports from other military men in the field, and echoed by governors in Kansas and Nebraska, could not persuade Sheridan, Belknap, or other Washington officials of the legitimacy of the requests or of the government's duty to act. If this had been the first time that the army had been called upon to supply military stores to victims of natural disaster, the reticence of the officials might be more credible. Then, indeed, they might have had cause to worry about whether, as Ord promised, Congress would ratify the distribution. But this was not the first time.

Only a year earlier, in April 1874, Congress had approved an appropriation of almost six hundred thousand dollars in food and clothing—much of it military stores—for victims of the Mississippi River flood. The situation was similar; the fund was intended to "prevent starvation and suffering and extreme want to any and all classes of destitute or helpless persons living on or near the Lower Mississippi River, who have been rendered so by reason of the present overflow of the Mississippi River." One of the arguments then used to sway the Senate was that such an appropriation lay "in the line of precedents." Another precedent for federal involvement had occurred under General Sheridan's personal supervision. In 1871 he did not hesitate to help the victims of the Chicago fire. He took charge of the city to protect it against looting and anarchy. The army issued about three hundred thousand rations and thousands of blankets and tents. And, when Sheridan realized that aid would be required through the winter, he encouraged President Grant to approve long-term assistance for the victims. When Sheridan himself could see the needy and was in control of relief efforts, he showed sympathy and compassion. When, however, he sat at some distance and had no firsthand knowledge of the plight of the sufferers, he did not exhibit the same willingness to help.[20]

Ord found his most sympathetic backer in Senator Hitchcock of Omaha. In December, Hitchcock tried to guide through Congress a bill authorizing the distribution of one hundred thousand dollars in army food, an amount suggested by Ord. Although the bill received favorable action in the Senate Committee on Military Affairs, it did not become law in 1874.[21]

The Departments of the Platte, under Ord, and of the Missouri, commanded by General John Pope, distributed clothing throughout the winter of 1874–75. But the Department of the Dakota, commanded by General Alfred Terry and headquartered in St. Paul, did not. In early January the adjutant general instructed Ord and Pope to arrange issues in such a way "that the most perfect accountability may be established." Previous allotments, he wrote, "have caused scandal in the Congress" because of the irresponsibility of management. Since the President took responsibility for authorizing distribution and hoped for congressional approval, he wanted the supplies given out carefully.[22]

Finally, in early February 1875, both houses of Congress granted $150,000 to relieve grasshopper sufferers and to pay for earlier issues

116

of clothing. Representative Stephen A. Cobb of Kansas, who introduced the bill, displayed the boosterism common among politicians in the afflicted areas. He confessed that this bill offended his pride, but the necessity of the situation compelled him to sponsor it. "This relief . . . is the only means to save many of my people from the horrors of death by starvation and exposure." Private relief, although generous, just could not fill the need. And, he reassured the House, the people could not be found at fault. "The act of God alone could reduce us to this extremity."[23]

To stress the necessity for the appropriation, Cobb read aloud a letter from General Ord. His letter, which used both his military and civilian titles, described the conditions, the inadequate private efforts, and the need for federal assistance. Ord insisted that the government bore an absolute responsibility to help. "These people," he wrote, "have been largely induced by donations of Government lands to settle where they now are, and have also been promised assistance in their distress if they would remain. . . . their lands are valuable, the country healthy and productive, and with a little aid from the Government in this their hour of need they will gladly remain and become useful citizens." The House approved the bill by more than three to one. The vote followed party and sectional lines. Republicans overwhelmingly favored the bill; only three cast negative votes. The Democrats split almost exactly — forty-six opposed and forty-eight approved (of the forty-eight, most came from western states). Three days later the Senate approved by voice vote. Then, on February 10, 1875, the President signed the bill and it became law.

The War Department wasted no time in implementing the law. On February 12 the adjutant general issued a general order outlining the method of enrollment of the destitute and of determining distribution points. It was only then that the Department of the Dakota, under General Terry, became involved in relief efforts. Terry did as the department ordered, but not much more. In early December 1874, the *Martin County Sentinel* asked: "Why should not Minnesota receive her share of Government aid?" No one replied. But General Terry's inaction doubtlessly contributed to the minimum involvement of the army in the Department of the Dakota — both before and after the congressional appropriation.[24]

On February 16, the date Terry received his orders from the War Department, he sent a letter to Governor Davis that displayed

117

amazing ignorance of conditions in the state. Few issues had so occupied the attention of the *St. Paul Pioneer Press* during the mid-1870s as the grasshopper infestations. Yet, Terry knew little of the situation. "I do not know the parts of the state in which such destitution exists," he wrote, "but I am aware that your Excellency has given much attention to the subject that I therefore respectfully request that you will give me whatever information in regard to it may be in your possession." Five days later Terry assigned several men to visit the affected areas and to enroll the destitute. He directed the officers to work through county officials to determine the merits of the applicants.[25]

During late February and early March, the officers traveled throughout southwestern Minnesota and southeastern Dakota Territory compiling lists of needy people. In Brown County Lieutenant J. M. Burns enrolled about four hundred families, a figure that surprised Terry. "The Department Commander has no idea there can be so many . . . really requiring aid," Terry's assistant informed Burns, "he expects you to sift the applications well and with discretion." A few days later department headquarters directed another officer in the field to limit his attention to those who had suffered grasshopper losses and stipulated the qualifications for relief: "Those who are earning a fair support or who can do so by work in the vicinity of their homes are not proper subjects for this relief and must not be enrolled." In late March, the list completed, Terry reported that almost nine thousand in Minnesota and just over five thousand in Dakota Territory needed help. To supply these people the department received 18 percent — twenty-seven thousand dollars — of the appropriation. Terry allowed each adult one pound of flour and half a pound of bacon; for a child under twelve, half a ration.[26]

The *Pioneer Press* kept careful watch over the project and cheerfully reported, "Thus far no cases of actual suffering from want of food have been reported." Nor did the soldiers find any pressing need for clothing or flour. In fact, the paper editorialized, probably more city people required help than did the frontier settlers. After the completion of the canvass, the *Pioneer Press* assumed an openly skeptical position. It reported that foreign-born settlers, primarily, had requested aid. While "Americans" faced severe losses and great need, they declined to apply; their pride kept them from throwing themselves on public charity. The newspaper also charged that many of the applicants found themselves in want not because of the grasshoppers but through their own fault. "They came into the State poor, and have remained so, either from bad management or constitutional laziness." Many who applied could certainly care for themselves without outside help. The *Pioneer Press* did not condemn the issue of government rations but did question its necessity, stressing again that no cases of "utter destitution" existed in either Minnesota or Dakota.[27]

General Terry agreed. As he reported to the secretary of war at the end of the year: "The officers in charge of the enrollment and of the issue of supplies became, during their intercourse with the people, strongly impressed with the belief that the representations which had been made in regard to the amount of loss and suffering caused by grasshopper ravages were greatly exaggerated. . . ." Of more concern to Terry, "there is too much reason to fear that many who received the aid of the Government secured their enrollment by false pretenses notwithstanding the conscientious effort which was made to prevent such fraud." Not surprisingly, the *Pioneer Press* quoted this report verbatim.[28]

While the *Pioneer Press*, Terry, and some of the enrolling officers may have recorded what they saw, numerous county officials observed something else. Warren Smith of Heron Lake complained to Sibley: "The U.S. Government in making the enrollment, for unexplainable reasons, left out many families who are amongst the most worthy and needy of the sufferers, and as the State Relief has been discontinued they are suffering extremely." In general, the commissioners in Smith's county thought the supply "scanty and insufficient." A commissioner in Brown County asked Davis "what has become of the U.S. Government Relief . . . nothing has reached our County. . . ." The auditor of Nobles County also inquired about federal relief. "I write to say that quite a number of the destitute who were enrolled [in the county] . . . have by some means been dropped off the list and among these are some of the most needy in the county." Others who were equally worthy, in the commissioners' estimation, were never included at all on the list. And the chairman of the Martin County commissioners complained: "Many were left out who are as needy as those who received."[29]

No doubt some farmers misrepresented their cases and received assistance that they did not actually require. Yet the reports from county officials cannot be dismissed as wild exaggerations or simple attempts to defraud the government. Nor can the numerous appeals to the governor from individuals describing their plight be categorized as intentionally misleading. A Renville County man who wrote that he had no means to buy seed or provisions and was "naked of clothing" or the Jackson County man who had "no meat nor groceries nor nothing to get any more with" were probably not being deceitful. Either the army officers or the *Pioneer Press* lacked an accurate picture of conditions, or they and county officials and victims held substantially different definitions of need and "utter destitution."[30]

Over 107,000 people, including about 44,000 children under the age of twelve, received government rations. That so many received food from an actual expended appropriation of $133,000 demonstrates that scant opportunity existed for farmers to defraud the federal government significantly.[31]

The three departments of the army stationed in the West — the Platte, the Missouri, and the Dakota — shared the congressional appropriation, but not equally. The portion for each depended upon the enrollments. No single set of rules determined the qualifications for relief; each department made its own. A skeptical commanding general or an overly generous one easily influenced the definition of eligibility. The Department of the Dakota enrolled substantially fewer settlers than the other two departments, but it is not clear that the Dakota contained fewer actual victims.

The Missouri received the largest share of the appropriation — sixty-three thousand dollars. Of that amount, it spent 90 percent on rations, 8 percent on operating costs, and returned 2 percent to the federal treasury. The Platte received forty-eight thousand dollars and expended an even higher proportion on actual rations — 92 percent, while using only 6 percent for expenses and returning 3 percent. The Department of the Dakota, however, made the smallest expenditure on rations — 72 percent. It spent, as well, the most, proportionately, on expenses — 17 percent — and returned the largest percentage to the federal treasury — 10 percent. These figures may testify to the difficulty of distributing supplies in the Dakota. They might also suggest that Terry, in spite of his serious concern about settlers defrauding the government, operated his department with the least efficiency of the three.

Without Ord's dedicated, persistent, and assiduous efforts, it is doubtful that the federal government would have become involved in any way in direct relief. General Sheridan openly opposed the procedure. General Pope exerted little energy to draw federal funds. General Terry displayed scant interest and much suspicion of the entire plan. Ord wrote letters and sent telegrams; he actively supported the congressional bills. He effectively combined his responsibilities as relief chairman of the Nebraska Relief and Aid Association with those he had as commanding general of the Department of the Platte. Unfortunately for grasshopper victims throughout the West, the War Department transferred Ord to Texas in mid-March 1875. His removal from Omaha left the stricken settlers without a sympathetic and persuasive spokesman. By the middle of May, the appropriation had been expended; this ended the official involvement of the United States Army in frontier relief.[32]

The last effort of the federal government falls more correctly into the category of long-term assistance, not of relief. In October 1876, at the invitation of John S. Pillsbury, the governors of Iowa, Kansas, Missouri, Nebraska, and Dakota Territory met in Omaha to devise a "comprehensive plan" and to secure a "concert of action . . . which might prove in some degree commensurate with the magnitude of the evil to be encountered." Pillsbury was elected president of the convention, and in his opening remarks he set the guidelines and called upon the agrarian myth. His first goal was to involve the federal government. The locusts presented a menace with which no single state or community could "cope successfully." By attacking agriculture, the backbone of the nation, the plague "threatens the source of productive industry. . . ." If the government believed itself responsible for facilitating the movement of crops by improving rivers and harbors and by promoting internal commerce, Pillsbury stated, "surely the rescue of those crops from destruction is no less an object of its rightful care." The governors approved of this emphasis on federal assistance and shared the sentiments of Governor C. H. Hardin of Missouri, who argued, "few objects could afford a more legitimate field for the exercise of its [federal] power."[33]

The governors called for a federally funded investigation "into the history and habits of this insect . . . and the search for all possible means of its extermination. . . ." Rather than requesting a separate piece of legislation, the governors proposed to add a clause to the

Sundry Civil Appropriation bill making an appropriation for the Geological and Geographic Survey of the Territories: "And also the further sum of twenty-five thousand dollars for the purpose of paying the salaries and expenses of a commission to consist of three entomologists and two Western men who have had experience with the locusts, to be appointed by the Chief of said survey, with the consent and approval of the Secretary of the Interior."[34]

The particular form of the proposal and its request that the commission be attached to the geological and geographic survey resulted from careful and painstaking negotiation, but little of it happened at the governors' conference. Two of the main actors in the proceedings played an active role in the conference; two others watched carefully from a distance. Cyrus Thomas and Charles V. Riley, state entomologists of Missouri and Illinois, respectively, attended the meeting, partly because of their extensive knowledge of the Rocky Mountain locust; they were the undisputed experts in the field. But they wanted, too, to guarantee the passage of their entomological commission proposal. The other two figures in the drama were Ferdinand V. Hayden, chief of the Geological and Geographic Survey of the Territories, and Alfred Packard, Massachusetts state entomologist. Both Packard and Thomas had worked for Hayden in the survey during the early 1870s. Riley, a long-time supporter of congressional funding for the study of "injurious insects," had in early 1876 collaborated with Hayden on an entomological commission bill that died in congressional committee. Thomas had previously worked to increase national understanding of the Rocky Mountain locust. His appeals to the Department of Agriculture, however, had received no action.[35]

All three of the state entomologists wanted to be members of the commission. They also shared an antipathy for the type of entomology then current in the federal government. They favored "practical" or what Cyrus Thomas called "economic entomology" — entomology that involved active field work rather than book knowledge and emphasized protection against injurious insects as opposed to describing new species. Their preferences account for their desire to attach the commission to the geological and geographic survey rather than to the Department of Agriculture. The entomological division of the Department of Agriculture had been founded in 1863. Since then an entomologist, Townsend Glover, plus one clerical assistant, had handled all its business. Because of limited personnel, but, more importantly, because of inclination, the two men confined themselves primarily to desk research in their Washington, D.C., office. The division epitomized and Glover personified the impractical entomology condemned by Thomas, Packard, and Riley. As Thomas complained to Hayden, "you might as well try to get a prairie dog out of his hole as to get Glover out of his nest." He continued, "I had to get appointed to the Conference of Governors so as to bring up the matter."[36]

The proposal, supported by the western governors through a memorial to Congress and the intercession of their representatives, plus the work of Thomas, Riley, Packard, and Hayden, received favorable action. On March 3, 1877, President Rutherford B. Hayes approved an appropriation for a three man entomological commission attached to the geological and geographic survey, charged "to report upon the depredations of the Rocky Mountain locusts in the Western States and Territories and the best practicable methods of preventing their recurrence, or guarding against their invasions." Two weeks later Secretary of the Interior Carl Schurz appointed Riley, Packard, and Thomas to the United States Entomological Commission. Riley became chairman and he established headquarters in St. Louis, Missouri, appropriately enough on Locust Street.[37]

The commission worked expeditiously to carry out its mandate. The members did extensive field work, distributed "how-to" pamphlets, tapped the United States Signal Corps to watch the insects on the wing, and published several substantial volumes in 1878 and 1880 encompassing all they had learned. By the time most of the information was collected, analyzed, and published, the grasshoppers no longer threatened western crops.[38]

The entomological commission came into being because a few men — Thomas, in particular — took personal responsibility for securing federal assistance. All three entomologists possessed impeccable credentials, and they aimed at more than the study of Rocky Mountain locusts. They wanted to refocus the activities of the federal government in the area of entomological research, and the depredations of the grasshoppers provided the opportunity to press their requests. This convergence of opportunity and motive resulted in a successful concerted effort.

The amount of federal assistance extended to sufferers of the grasshopper plagues in the 1870s constituted, in nineteenth-century terms, a substantial and unusual effort. Extensions of deadlines and distribution of seed followed federal practice for involvement in the aid of disaster sufferers. Allotment of army food and clothing, while not unprecedented, did not come easily. Only Ord's personal commitment brought about federal involvement. Dissatisfaction with the entomological division of the Department of Agriculture, and the active dedication of Cyrus Thomas and others to the establishment of an entomological commission, resulted in federal backing. The federal assistance, while well intended, offered too little, too late, and produced mixed results. Perhaps the relative unfamiliarity of the government with direct relief prevented it from doing more. Perhaps nineteenth-century concepts about federal responsibility and about the causes of distress limited what the executive and legislative branches believed to be proper procedures. But lawmakers of every level had taken some initial steps.

———

The grasshopper plagues of the mid-1870s provide an introduction to individuals as different as Mary Carpenter and John S. Pillsbury. The infestations lead to contemplation of the nearly crushing difficulties of nineteenth-century farming, the despair of watching one's work and income, sometimes the future, devoured by pests no bigger than a woman's thumb. The plagues draw attention to the helplessness, sometimes the reluctance, of county governments to aid their citizens; to state officials disagreeing about policy; to one military officer oblivious to the needy around him and another painfully aware and moved to act; to scientists who recognized a chance to correct the misdirection of federal research in entomology. These elements alone constitute a fascinating period in agricultural, rural, Minnesota, midwestern, and western history.

The plagues bear a larger significance, as well, in American social history. They reflect the role of farmers and they highlight the changing values in American society. The poverty and need occasioned by the plagues brought two central values of American culture into direct conflict — the nobility of farmers and the work ethic. Farmers needed help, relief, and charity. Were they not noble? Did poverty result from forces other than the moral failing of the poor? Both values could not be honored when they clashed so directly. Either the special status of farmers or the money ethic (in the guise of the work ethic) had to yield.

In 1871 the Chicago fire left thousands of people in need. This disaster elicited sympathy and assistance from a benevolent public and aid from city, state, and federal governments. The same General Sheridan who later hardly noticed the grasshopper plagues quickly provided military assistance — tents, blankets, food, protection from looters — for fire victims. Professional charity workers worried little that individuals would be corrupted by gifts, since the fire was accidental. People in Chicago suffered from the fire, but rarely from accusations of paupery or personal failing. Certainly they did not bear responsibility for their condition.

Yet, when midwestern farmers faced natural disaster, not once, but as many as five times in succession, they only intermittently captured the sympathy of the nation. They were more often seen as "the poor." Farm families, treated as if they had somehow caused or at least contributed to their losses, felt themselves mistrusted, their character questioned. Their hard work, diligence, even their reputed virtue neither brought them success nor shielded them from suspicion of taking advantage of public generosity. The charitable worried about the hazard of encouraging dependence and lack of initiative in farmers.

The Minnesota legislature, acting out these attitudes, saddled relief appropriations with extensive restraints to prevent the unworthy from benefiting. The state went so far as to require from the needy farmers a version of the pauper's oath. These "safeguards" limited the amount distributed and served as a weightier hindrance to giving out relief than the size of the state budget.

Governor Cushman K. Davis tempered these attitudes, pointing to the state's concern for retaining settlers. But suspicion gained power under the leadership of Governor John S. Pillsbury. A devotee of New England thinking about the evils of charity, himself never a farmer but a miller of grain, he frowned on charity for the able-bodied, as if able bodies protected wheat fields from insects. He preferred to encourage farmers' independence by offering loans rather than gifts. In the tradition of patrician philanthropists of the late nineteenth century, he looked for private contributions, and he personally supervised the distribution of assistance. His hope was to preserve the dignity of farmers; his effect was to deny it.

While the charitable suspected farm people and worried about their moral state, farmers, of course, did not suspect themselves. No doubt they shared American attitudes about the unworthy poor. They, too, would deny help to those who refused to work. But farm people knew that they were not guilty of malingering. They knew that they were industrious; they just did not have enough money or luck.

Response to the grasshopper plagues belied the cultural value attached to farmers and demonstrated that the money ethic would win out in this cultural conflict. The response serves as a barometer of the declining value of farmers in American society and the increasing value of money. Success would come to be measured more by wealth than by nobility of occupation.

Farmers survived the 1870s without feeling the full effects of this change. When relative prosperity returned to agriculture in the early 1880s and farm people had less need to seek outside assistance, the conflict in values receded temporarily. But the hard times of the late 1880s and 1890s sharpened the contrast and the conflict. If urban people felt little sympathy for farmers in the 1870s, they felt less in the 1890s.

The balance of population continued to shift from farms and small villages to towns and cities. The frontier, declared Frederick Jackson Turner and the superintendent of the census, closed with the 1890 census. The 1893 Columbian Exposition at which Turner announced this "fact" occurred in Chicago, the heartland of the nation and the agrarian center of the United States. The fair, however, did not celebrate its agricultural setting nor particularly honor America as a farming nation. The planning committee included an agricultural building, to be sure, but the concept of the fair, its guiding ideas, were decidedly nonagricultural, even antiagricultural. The White City, the classical architecture, the Romanesque statues, the central Italianate pool – all reflected a vision of a new, urban America.

If at the beginning of the 1870s industrialists and big businessmen threatened to unseat farmers from their place in national culture and esteem, the overthrow largely took place by the 1890s. Certainly Americans continued and today still continue to give lip service to the nobility of farmers and now to its twentieth-century version, the family farm. But what did farmers have to offer in an increasingly cash-based and money-conscious society? What did nobility count against bank receipts?

The mythic noble yeoman was good and moral, but never necessarily rich. Barter – the everyday currency of many farms – or egg money, garden produce, quilting bees, neighborhood threshings, and barn raisings might provide some people with satisfying and emotionally rich lives, but did not furnish much money to match the cash of industrialists and white-collar workers. Neighborhood parties and dances, church suppers and school doings brought their own rewards, but they lacked the thrill and dazzle and lights of the city. What farm people had to offer was not in much demand.

In the 1870s farmers asked for assistance; they appealed as equals to their equals. Instead, they got charity, gifts from superior to inferior. By the 1890s farmers, aware of their declining status, no longer asked. They organized and demanded. To gain equality, they looked more determinedly to politics and to their own parties. They less often cited their nobility but more often stressed their economic contributions to society. They, too, changed their thinking about themselves and their roles. They, too, accepted the money ethic. Unfortunately for them, the money ethic has never fit a rural setting. When farmers accepted the money ethic, they did not assure their own success. More likely, they assured their continued decline in American society.

In the cultural conflict between the farmers' nobility and the money ethic, farmers were set aside. American ideas about them changed; ideas about poverty did not. The poor continued to suffer economically and ideologically because they lacked money. They continued to be held personally responsible for their conditions. In the 1930s Franklin D. Roosevelt's New Deal and in the 1960s Lyndon B. Johnson's Great Society took steps, but only small ones, toward blaming the victim less and the system more. Money continues to measure success and poverty to measure failure.

Reference Notes

The sources for this study are rich ones. Virtually no Minnesota settler whose papers have survived from the 1870s fails to mention the impact of the grasshoppers. These papers, held in the Division of Archives and Manuscripts of the Minnesota Historical Society (abbreviated as DAM-MHS), offer a personal and individual view invaluable to this work. The Governor's Papers in the Minnesota State Archives (also in DAM-MHS) contain virtually nothing by the governors themselves but include hundreds of letters from settlers, county and town commissioners, and formal and informal organizations. Most of the letter writers ask for help. Others describe relief procedures or conditions in a particular area. Some criticize the manner of assistance or form of distribution. A few relay reports of neighbors or other settlers receiving too much or too little. Clearly, these people do not represent a cross section of the state's population, but they do tell a side of the story unavailable elsewhere.

The Henry Hastings Sibley Papers include correspondence and reports for the state relief committee that Sibley chaired. These proved helpful. In 1949 *The Farmer* magazine invited subscribers who had lived in the state fifty or more years to write to the magazine, sending their memories and stories. Expecting to receive several dozen, the editorial staff was overwhelmed by the hundreds of accounts that flooded in. The magazine published only a few of the letters and then gave the entire file to the Minnesota Historical Society. Many of the letter writers recall stories of the grasshopper days.

Official records tell another side. I depended heavily on Minnesota statutes, journals of the state senate and house of representatives, and reports of state officials. The reports of the commissioner of statistics, auditor, and the University of Minnesota, as well as the annual messages of the governors, are published yearly as *Minnesota Executive Documents*; they are cited by agency and year.

I also used papers held in the National Archives in Washington, D.C. They are organized and categorized into numbered Record Groups; the collections are abbreviated as NARG. I made most use of the Records of the United States Entomological Commission (NARG 48), the Geological and Geographic Survey of the Territories (Hayden Survey) (NARG 57), the Quartermaster General (NARG 92), the Adjutant General (NARG 94), the Secretary of War (NARG 107), and the Army Continental Commands (NARG 393).

Newspapers also reported and editorialized extensively about the activities of governments and settlers. The *St. Paul Pioneer Press* (which went through several name changes during the 1870s) was particularly useful.

Few counties kept official correspondence, but they have preserved land, tax, and mortgage records. Chippewa County officials saved county records of grasshopper relief. Both Martin and Chippewa counties preserved minutes of commissioners' meetings, budgets, and expenditures. For county activities, the *Martin County Sentinel* (Fairmont) and the wealth of published county histories also proved helpful. I did not attempt a comprehensive survey of county records except in Chippewa and Martin counties, which were different enough in age, population composition, ethnicity, and farming practices to provide different examples. But they resemble each other and surrounding counties enough to allow for generalization. It should be noted that Minnesota had seventy-six counties in the years 1873–78 — eleven less than the state has at the present.

Official records tended to use accepted spelling and grammar. Letters from farmers, however, are full of idiosyncratic usages. I have kept the original forms and inserted "*sic*" into the text only when the sense of the originals is unclear.

I have also made extensive use of novels. Like the personal papers, virtually every novel set in the Midwest in the late-nineteenth century includes direct and indirect information about the plagues. However fictional in characterization and plot, the novels portrayed the conditions in ways that not only confirmed what I found in other sources, but also enriched it.

The secondary literature on agriculture, charity, relief, social welfare, disasters, farm life, and social conditions in the nineteenth century is extensive. Gilbert C. Fite's work on the plagues offered more help than the notes can suggest. For a complete bibliography, see my doctoral dissertation, "Everything But the Mortgage: The Response to Agricultural Disaster in Minnesota, 1873–1878" (Ph.D. thesis, Indiana University, 1981).

Three books helped me particularly, though in widely different ways. Daniel T. Rodgers, *The Work Ethic in Industrial America, 1850–1920* (Chicago, 1978), helped me think about work and poverty and values in the nineteenth century. Kai T. Erickson, *Everything in Its Path: Destruction of Community in the Buffalo Creek Flood* (New York, 1976), gave me clues about the impact of disasters on individuals and communities. And Donald Worster, *The Dust Bowl: The Southern Plains in the 1930s* (New York, 1979), taught me by example to write a story at the same time that I wrote a historical monograph.

Preface

[1] John T. Schlebecker, "Grasshoppers in American Agricultural History," in *Agricultural History*, 27:85–93 (July, 1953).

Chapter 1. *A Value System Threatened*

[1] Kai T. Erikson, *Everything in Its Path: Destruction and Community in the Buffalo Creek Flood*, 81 (New York, 1976).

[2] Sherry B. Ortner, "On Key Symbols," in *American Anthropologist*, 1338–1346 (1973); Leon Festinger, *A Theory of Cognitive Dissonance* (Evanston, Ill., 1957).

[3] Thomas Jefferson, *Notes on the State of Virginia*, ed. by William Peden, 164 (Chapel Hill, N.C., 1954).

[4] Much of this chapter grows out of my reading of Daniel T. Rodgers' fascinating and provocative book about the work ethic and changing values resulting from industrialization in the nineteenth century; see Rodgers, *The Work Ethic in Industrial America, 1850–1920* (Chicago, 1978) (quotations, xi, 12).

[5] See, for example, Horatio Alger, Jr., *Ragged Dick and Mark, the Match Boy*, intro. by Richard Fink (Reprint ed., New York, 1962).

[6] David Rothman, *The Discovery of the Asylum: Social Order and Disorder in the New Republic* (Boston, 1971).

[7] Clarke Chambers to author, January 21, 1982, in author's possession.

Chapter 2. *Plague: The Grasshoppers Arrive*

[1] Gilbert C. Fite, *The Farmers' Frontier, 1865–1900*, 55 (New York, 1966). Fite devotes a chapter to "Destitution on the Frontier in the 1870s" in which he outlines the major hardships and the variety of government efforts in several states to come to the assistance of the settlers. Fite also edited a short collection of letters from distressed settlers to the governors of Minnesota; see, Gilbert C. Fite, ed., "Some Farmers' Accounts of Hardship on the Frontier," in *Minnesota History*, 37:204–211 (March, 1961).

[2] United States Dept. of the Interior, Geological Survey, *Report of the Entomological Commission for 1877*, 55–113 (Washington, D.C., 1878); hereafter cited as U.S. Geological Survey, *Report, 1877*.

[3] Here and three paragraphs below, see U.S. Geological Survey, *Report, 1877*, 31–52, 114, 118–121.

[4] O. E. Rölvaag, *Giants in the Earth: A Saga of the Prairie*, 340, 341 (New York, 1927).

[5] Josephine Barry Donovan, "Grasshopper Times," in *Palimpsest*, 4:194 (June, 1923); Laura Ingalls Wilder, *On the Banks of Plum Creek*, 194, 260 (Reprint ed., New York, 1971); Edward Ellsworth Gillam to Ruth Thompson, March 21, 1949, Ruth Thompson Papers; Edward Mohagen, *The Farmer* Collection; J. W. Powell, "A Short Sketch of Frontier Work in Southwestern Minnesota," paper prepared for the Methodist Historical Society, Minnesota, June 5, 1900, Methodist Episcopal Church, Minnesota Annual Conference Historical Society Papers — all DAM-MHS.

[6] Edward Mohagen, *The Farmer* Collection; Knute Steenerson Reminiscences (reprinted in "Knute Steenerson's Recollections: The Story of a Pioneer," in *Minnesota History Bulletin*, 4:130–151 [August-November, 1921]); Mrs. Alvin Lia, *The Farmer*

Collection; "LBR" to "Friend Atwood," August 5, 1876, Edwin H. Atwood and Family Papers; Mrs. Louis Anderson, Mabel Larson, *The Farmer* Collection — all in DAM-MHS.

[7]Mrs. Peter Schechter, Mrs. W. Kreuger, *The Farmer* Collection; *St. Paul Daily Pioneer*, July 29, 1873.

[8]*St. Paul Daily Pioneer*, July 2, 1873; James Christie to Alex Christie, June 29, 1873, James C. Christie and Family Papers, DAM-MHS.

[9]Here and two paragraphs below, see Maud Lovelace and Delos Lovelace, *Gentlemen from England*, 55–67 (New York, 1937).

[10]Minnesota Commissioner of Statistics, *Reports*, 1874, p. 8–10. All statements of losses are estimates that indicate the difference between what was produced and what the commissioner calculated would have been produced had there been no grasshopper infestations. The percentages were computed by the author from data in the annual reports of the commissioner of statistics. See also Merrill E. Jarchow, *The Earth Brought Forth: A History of Minnesota Agriculture to 1885*, 165–187 (St. Paul, 1949).

[11]*Worthington Western Advance*, July 18, 1874.

[12]William Bird, Jr., to Cushman K. Davis, June 2, 13, Edward F. Wade to Davis, June 28, Leonard Aldrich to Davis, June 3 — all 1874, in Governor's Papers, DAM-MHS.

[13]*St. Paul Daily Pioneer*, July 8, 9, 1874; *Worthington Western Advance*, July 18, 1874.

[14]E. F. Jackson to Davis, June 15, H. S. Austin to Davis, June 24 — both 1874, in Governor's Papers.

[15]Commissioner of Statistics, *Reports*, 1875, p. 18, 19; Johanna Kragh, Andrew Stenerson, Selma Swenson — all in *The Farmer* Collection.

[16]*St. Paul Sunday Pioneer*, July 19, 1874.

[17]Commissioner of Statistics, *Reports*, 1876, p. 860–863.

[18]*St. Paul and Minneapolis Pioneer Press and Tribune*, May 24, June 14, May 5, 1876.

[19]Commissioner of Statistics, *Reports*, 1877, p. 19–30, 88–93.

[20]Pauline Farseth and Theodore C. Blegen, trans. and eds., *Frontier Mother: The Letters of Gro Svendsen*, 130, 131 (Northfield, 1950); Charles V. Riley, *Ninth Annual Report of the Noxious, Beneficial, and Other Insects of the State of Missouri*, 122 (Jefferson City, Mo., 1877); *St. Paul Daily Pioneer Press*, May 18, 1877; U.S. Geological Survey, *Report*, 1877, 86.

[21]"Geological and Natural History Survey of Minnesota," in University of Minnesota, *Reports*, 1877, p. 870–882.

[22]Ole K. Broste Reminiscences, George G. Barnum Reminiscences — both in DAM-MHS.

[23]Emma C. White Reminiscences, DAM-MHS.

[24]David R. Breed, *The Locust-Scourge in Minnesota*, 13, 14, 16, 18 (New York, 1878).

[25]Abram M. Fridley and Family Papers, DAM-MHS.

Chapter 3. *The Farmers React*

[1]Mrs. W. Krueger, *The Farmer* Collection; John Ise, *Sod and Stubble: The Story of a Kansas Homestead*, 50 (New York, 1936); Rölvaag, *Giants in the Earth*, 345; Hjalmar Rued Holand, *Norwegians in America: The Last Migration*, ed. by Evelyn Ostraat Wierenga, trans. by Helmer M. Blegen, 188 (Sioux Falls, S.Dak., 1978);

131

Laura Hilden Hanson and Rose Linda Carney, both in *The Farmer* Collection; Martha Ostenso, *O River, Remember!*, 182–185 (New York, 1943); Gertrude B. Vandergon, *Our Pioneer Days in Minnesota*, 102 (N.p., 1949); William J. Davidson, "Minnesota — Ox-Cart to Airplane," pamphlet, William J. Davidson Papers; James H. Quinn, "Some Early Minnesota History from the Autobiography of Judge James H. Quinn," James H. Quinn Papers — both DAM-MHS.

² *St. Paul Daily Pioneer Press*, May 25, 27, 1877; Emma C. White Reminiscences; R. Douglas Hurt, "Grasshopper Harvesters on the Great Plains," in *Great Plains Journal*, 16:123–134 (Spring, 1977); George H. Smith, Alfred Carsted, *The Farmer* Collection.

³ George Winthrop Lewis, "Sketch of the Life and Work of Martin B. Lewis and His Son," Biography File, DAM-MHS; "Geological and Natural History Survey of Minnesota," in University of Minnesota, *Reports*, 1877, p. 875, 876; *St. Paul Daily Pioneer Press*, June 23, 1877.

⁴ John A. Brown, ed., *History of Cottonwood and Watonwan Counties, Minnesota: Their People, Industries and Institutions*, 1:323 (Indianapolis, 1916); Isaac G. Haycraft Reminiscences, DAM-MHS; G. S. Thompson to Davis, May 19, 1874, J. T. Smith to Davis, May 20, 1874, Warren Smith to Davis, May 27, 1875 — all in Governor's Papers.

⁵ Rölvaag, *Giants in the Earth*, 353; Bess S. Aldrich, *A Lantern in Her Hand*, 74 (Reprint ed., New York, 1959).

⁶ *St. Paul Daily Pioneer*, July 2, 1873; Edward F. Wade to Davis, June 14, 1874, Edward Savage to Davis, June 22, 1874 — both in Governor's Papers.

⁷ P. J. Kniss to H. H. Sibley, August 25, 1874, H. H. Smith to John S. Pillsbury, October 3, 1876, Warren Smith to James Wakefield, July 27, 1876, William Sugar to Pillsbury, March 2, 1877 — all in Governor's Papers; *Martin County Sentinel* (Fairmont), August 7, 1874; Aldrich, *A Lantern in Her Hand*.

⁸ *Minneapolis Star and Tribune*, April 2, 1984, p. 3B, 7B.

⁹ Commissioner of Statistics, *Reports*, 1873, p. 514, 1875, p. 130, 131.

¹⁰ For studies of population mobility, see Stephan Thernstrom, *The Other Bostonians: Poverty and Progress in the American Metropolis, 1880–1970*, 220–230 (Cambridge, Mass., 1973); Stephan Thernstrom and Peter R. Knights, "Men in Motion: Some Data and Speculations about Urban Population Mobility in Nineteenth Century America," in *Journal of Interdisciplinary History*, 1:1–34 (Autumn, 1970); James C. Malin, "The Turnover of Farm Population in Kansas," in *Kansas Historical Quarterly*, 4:339–372 (November, 1935); Allan G. Bogue, *From Prairie to Corn Belt: Farming on the Illinois and Iowa Prairies in the Nineteenth Century*, 19–28 (Chicago, 1963); Merle Curti, *The Making of an American Community: A Case Study of Democracy in a Frontier Community*, 65–77 (Stanford, Calif., 1959); Mildred Throne, "A Population Study of an Iowa County in 1850," in *Iowa Journal of History*, 57:305–330 (October, 1959).

¹¹ Register of (Initial) Homestead Entries, General Land Office Papers, DAM-MHS. Some of the decline reflected the effects of the depression of the mid-1870s and occurred in other parts of the United States.

¹² Here and two paragraphs below, see Mary Carpenter to Aunt Martha, July 10, 1873, Carpenter Papers, DAM-MHS.

¹³ Carpenter to Aunt Lucy, October 26, 1873, Carpenter Papers.

¹⁴ *Martin County Sentinel*, July 10, 24, 1874; T. S. Curtis to Davis, July 24, 1874, Mary Jones to David Jones, October 5, 1874 — both in Governor's Papers.

¹⁵ E. F. Jackson to Davis, July 21, 1875, Governor's Papers.

¹⁶ T. G. Carter to Secretary, Aetna Life Insurance Company, December 9, 1874, Carter to H. Lauplin, June 16, 1875, Carter to Cousin & Friends, August 9, 1875, Carter to A. W. Mircer, July 18, 1876, Carter to Bro. Samuel, August 28, 1876,

Carter to W. C. Gould, August 18, 1877 – all in vols. 4, 5, Letterbooks, Theodore G. Carter and Family Papers, DAM-MHS.

[17] Carter to Aetna Life Insurance Company, December 9, 1874, Carter to Bro. Samuel, August 28, 1876 – both in Carter Papers.

[18] Carter to Aetna Life Insurance Company, December 9, 1874, Carter to F. T. Day, January 24, 1875, Carter to Day, September 27, 1875, Carter to H. S. Durand, December 26, 1874, Carter to J. M. Hanks, November 5, 1875, Carter to Mircer, July 18, 1876 – all in Carter Papers.

[19] Carter to Durand, December 26, 1874, Carter to Lauplin, June 16, 1875 – both in Carter Papers.

[20] Carter to Cousin Electra, February 24, 1876, Carter to Hanks, November 5, 1875, Carter to E. H. S. Dart, May 15, 1875, Carter to A. O. E. Miller, June 17, 1875, Carter to Duvall McKenney, August 6, 1875, Carter to Parely, June 2, 1875 – all in Carter Papers.

[21] Carter to William R. Bloomfield, March 11, 1876, Carter to Bro. Samuel, August 28, 1876 – both in Carter Papers.

[22] Carter to Friend Butman, December 20, 1877, Carter to Mircer, January 7, 1878, Carter to Bro. Samuel, August 28, 1876 – all in Carter Papers.

[23] Thomas Williams to Davis, December 20, 1874, Governor's Papers; Carter to Friend Butman, February 26, 1878, Carter Papers; Mortgage Records, Office of Register of Deeds, Martin County Courthouse, Fairmont.

[24] Chattel Mortgage File Book, Tunsberg Township, Chippewa County Courthouse, Montevideo.

[25] Interview with Florence Conklin, July 30, 1979, Methodist Retirement Home, Fairmont, notes in author's possession; Commissioner of Statistics, *Reports*, 1873, p. 489–491, 1877, p. 95–97, 1878, p. 58–61.

[26] Commissioner of Statistics, *Reports*, 1873, p. 489, 1875, p. 65, 1877, p. 95, 1878, p. 58.

[27] "Assumption Chapel," leaflet (Cold Spring, 1952), in author's possession; Robert J. Voigt, *The Grasshopper Chapel* (St. Cloud, 1964). The chapel was built in 1877, destroyed by a tornado in 1894, and rebuilt in 1951.

[28] *Martin County Sentinel*, September 4, 1874; Henry B. Whipple, "Recollections of Persons and Events in the History of Minnesota," in *Minnesota Historical Collections*, 9:580 (St. Paul, 1901); J[acob] A. Kiester, *The History of Faribault County, Minnesota, from Its First Settlement to the Close of the Year 1879*, 366 (Minneapolis, 1896).

[29] Carpenter to Aunt Martha, July 10, 1873, Carpenter to Aunt Lucy, October 26, 1873 – both in Carpenter Papers.

[30] Reinhold Hummel to Dr. Dodin, October 13, 1874, Governor's Papers. Dodin, the St. Paul doctor, did not personally respond to the request but forwarded the letter to Governor Davis.

[31] John E. Miller to Davis, October 10, 1874, J. Milton Akers to Pillsbury, March 20, 1876 – both in Governor's Papers.

[32] Jennie Flint to Davis, February 6, 1874, John Laneby to Pillsbury, January 8, 1877 – both in Governor's Papers. Numerous other appeals to the governors are collected in the Governor's Papers. For petitions to legislators, see Minnesota, *House Journal*, 1874, p. 60, 68, and Minnesota, *Senate Journal*, 1874, p. 25, 33, 119, 145, 183, 238.

[33] Citizens of Saratoga, Lyon County, to Davis, [February, 1875], Governor's Papers.

[34] Mrs. T. Williams to Davis, February 9, 1875, S. D. Payne to Pillsbury, August 16, 1876, Citizens of Alba, Brown County, to Senate and House of Representatives, January 19, 1874 – all in Governor's Papers; *St. Paul Pioneer Press*, May 31, 1877.

³⁵Mary Jones to David Jones, October 5, 1874, Governor's Papers. Sometimes the values of self-sufficiency and independence gave way in the face of severe need. This pathetic letter from a pioneer woman to her husband survives because he sent it to Governor Davis. More moved by the plight of his wife and children than by the social norms discouraging relief, David Jones chose to beg. "I enclose a letter from my wife," he wrote to Davis, "and although it was not intended for other eyes than mine yet it may touch a sympathetic cord." The governor responded; a marginal note on the letter in Davis' hand reads: "Sent $18 to Mrs. Jones." D. Y. Jones to Davis, October 17, 1874, Governor's Papers.

³⁶P. F. Hunniston to Davis, July 24, 1874, A. A. Huntington to Davis, July 5, 1874 — both in Governor's Papers.

³⁷"The Address of the Martin County, Minnesota, Relief Committee," Governor's Papers. The appeal also appeared in the *Martin County Sentinel*, July 10, 1874.

³⁸Arthur P. Rose, *An Illustrated History of Nobles County, Minnesota*, 85 (Worthington, 1908).

³⁹J. W. Taylor to Davis, August 1, 1874, Governor's Papers.

Chapter 4. *Counties Face the Challenge*

¹Minnesota Territory, *Laws*, 1850, p. 128–130; Minnesota, *Statutes, Revised*, 1866, p. 201–207; Wisconsin Territory, *Statutes*, 1839, p. 132–135; Wisconsin, *Revised Statutes*, 1849; Elizabeth Gaspar Brown, "Poor Relief in a Wisconsin County, 1846–1866: Administration and Recipients," in *American Journal of Legal History*, 20:79–117 (April, 1976); Aileen E. Kennedy, *The Ohio Poor Law and Its Administration: A Study of Legislation in Rhode Island* (Chicago, 1936); Ralph E. Pumphrey and Muriel W. Pumphrey, eds., *The Heritage of American Social Work: Readings in Its Philosophical and Institutional Development* (New York, 1961); Rothman, *Discovery of the Asylum*; James Leiby, *A History of Social Welfare and Social Work in the United States* (New York, 1978); Robert H. Bremner, *From the Depths: The Discovery of Poverty in the United States* (New York, 1956); Robert H. Bremner, *The Public Good: Philanthropy and Welfare in the Civil War Era* (New York, 1980); Walter I. Trattner, *From Poor Law to Welfare State: A History of Social Welfare in America* (New York, 1974); Kathleen D. McCarthy, *Noblesse Oblige: Charity and Cultural Philanthropy in Chicago, 1849–1929* (Chicago, 1982).

²Robert H. Bremner, *American Philanthropy* (Chicago, 1960); Bremner, *From the Depths*; Daniel R. Noyes, "Charities in Minnesota," in *Minnesota Historical Collections*, 12:166–182 (St. Paul, 1908).

³Minutes of Meetings, January 6, 1874, Martin County Commissioners Record, Martin County Courthouse, Fairmont.

⁴Here and below, see "Citizens Meeting," February 11, 1874, unidentified newspaper clipping, Governor's Papers.

⁵Governor Cushman K. Davis and former Governor Henry Hastings Sibley, directing the state relief efforts, provided the impetus for these meetings by calling on individuals within the county to act. See Arthur P. Rose, *An Illustrated History of Jackson County, Minnesota*, 144, 145 (Jackson, 1910); "To the Supervisors and Clerks of Township [Nobles County]," undated circular, [December, 1873], Grasshopper Relief Committee, 1873–74, Correspondence and Miscellaneous Papers, Henry Hastings Sibley Papers, DAM-MHS.

⁶J. G. Redding to "Suffering Committee of Nobles County," [May 20, 1874], Governor's Papers.

⁷Minutes of Meeting at Windom, May 26, 1874, Governor's Papers.

[8]*Martin County Sentinel*, July 3, 1874.

[9]Ethel McClure, *More Than a Roof: The Development of Minnesota Poor Farms and Homes for the Aged*, 34 (St. Paul, 1968); M. B. Soule to Stephen Miller, July 2, 1874, Governor's Papers.

[10]Rose, *Nobles County*, 84.

[11]Ed[ward] F. Wade to Davis, July 5, 1874, Governor's Papers.

[12]Warren Smith to Sibley, December 23, 30, 1874, Governor's Papers.

[13]A. C. Hand to Davis, September 24, 1874, Governor's Papers.

[14]*Martin County Sentinel*, December 25, 1874.

[15]"To the Supervisors and Clerks of Township [Nobles County]," [1874], Sibley Papers; G. S. Thompson to Governor Davis, February 24, 1874, Governor's Papers.

[16]Minutes of Meeting at Windom, May 26, 1874, Governor's Papers; "Showing the No. of families No. of adults and Minors in each. No. of acres of different grain sown, in the County of Martin year ending May 1st 1874," Governor's Papers; Minnesota State Auditor, *Reports*, 1874, p. 80.

[17]A. W. Ward to Davis, July 9, 1874, Governor's Papers.

[18]*Martin County Sentinel*, July 31, October 2, 1874, January 15, June 11, 1875.

[19]Mrs. N. E. Davis to Sibley, February 13, 1875, A. E. West to Davis, August 12, 1874, J. W. Taylor to Davis, July 20, 1874, "Resolutions," Sleepy Eye, Brown County, [August 1, 1874] – all in Governor's Papers.

[20]Wade to Davis, December 20, 1874, Governor's Papers.

[21]*Martin County Sentinel*, September 4, 1874. This provision of too little time for those outside of the county seat to attend meetings happened more than once. On September 25 the *Sentinel* announced a meeting for October 3; on July 31, for August 8.

[22]Here and two paragraphs below, see *Martin County Sentinel*, October 2, 1874, January 15, June 11, 1875.

[23]Wade to Davis, December 20, 1874, January 3, 1875, Governor's Papers; *Martin County Sentinel*, October 2, 1874, January 15, June 11, 1875.

[24]J. D. Blake to Davis, January 4, 1875, Governor's Papers.

[25]T. S. Curtis to Sibley, December 21, 1874, Governor's Papers.

[26]Wade to Davis, February 19, 1875, Governor's Papers.

[27]Rose, *Nobles County*, 89; Commissioner of Statistics, *Reports*, 1875, p. 57, 59, 1876, p. 860; *Martin County Sentinel*, June 11, 1875.

[28]Meeker County Board of Commissioners to Davis, June, 1875, Governor's Papers; [John C. Wise, Warren Smith, and Allen Whitman], *The Grasshopper, or Rocky Mountain Locust, and Its Ravages in Minnesota: A Special Report to the Hon. C. K. Davis, Governor of Minnesota*, 44–46 (St. Paul, 1876); Minnesota, *Laws*, 1876, p. 116, 117.

Chapter 5. *The State Steps In*

[1]Here and below, see Minnesota, *Laws*, 1872, p. 165–167; Minnesota State Auditor, *Reports*, 1872, p. 370, 409.

[2]Address of Governor Horace Austin, March 5, 1873, *Executive Record*, vol. E, 110–112, Governor's Papers; Minnesota, *Laws*, 1873, p. 254, 272. Congress did not act on this recommendation.

[3]Address of Austin, March 5, 1873, *Executive Record*, vol. E, 112.

[4]Theodore C. Blegen, *Minnesota: A History of the State*, 133–140, 161–169, 214, 226, 278–281 ([Minneapolis], 1963); J. Fletcher Williams, "Henry Hastings Sibley: A Memoir," in *Minnesota Historical Collections*, 6:294, 298 (St. Paul, 1894). See also

Nathaniel West, *The Ancestry, Life, and Times of Hon. Henry Hastings Sibley, LL.D.* (St. Paul, 1889).

[5]*St. Paul Daily Pioneer*, December 23, 1873.

[6]*St. Paul Daily Pioneer*, December 24, 1873.

[7]*St. Paul Daily Pioneer*, December 25, 1873.

[8]H. T. Johns to Sibley, December 29, 1873, Sibley to H[enry] M. Rice, "Final Report of Relief Committee," June 27, 1874 – both in Sibley Papers. Red Wing sent almost $300; Faribault, $165; in addition to the county contribution of $200, the Winona citizens sent $150.

[9]*St. Paul Daily Pioneer*, December 27, 28, 1873.

[10]"Final Report of Relief Committee," June 27, 1874, Stephen Miller to Sibley, December 28, 30, 1873 – all in Sibley Papers.

[11]*St. Paul Daily Pioneer*, December 28, 1873; "Final Report of Relief Committee," June 27, 1874, Sibley Papers.

[12]"Final Report of Relief Committee," June 27, 1874, Sibley Papers.

[13]Horace Austin, "Annual Message," January 9, 1874, in Minnesota, *Executive Documents*, 1873, p. 26, 27.

[14]Cushman K. Davis, "Inaugural Message," January 9, 1874, in Minnesota, *Executive Documents*, 1873, p. 3, 4.

[15]*St. Paul Daily Pioneer*, January 25, 1874.

[16]Minnesota, *Laws*, 1874, p. 106, 251, 253, 286.

[17]*Senate Journal*, 1875, p. 101.

[18]Davis letter reprinted in Arthur P. Rose, *An Illustrated History of the Counties of Rock and Pipestone, Minnesota*, 80 (Luverne, 1911).

[19]State Auditor, *Reports*, 1874, p. 104; Minnesota Commission for the Relief of Sufferers, Executive Records, DAM-MHS. Prices for foodstuffs in 1874 ran ten cents a pound for pork and two and three-fourths cents a pound for flour; see Relief Receipts, 1874, Governor's Papers.

[20]George Overton to Davis, February 6, 7, 10, 12, 1874, Governor's Papers.

[21]P. J. Kniss to Davis, February 15, 1874, Eight Luverne Citizens to Davis, February 15, 1874 – both in Governor's Papers.

[22]Overton to Davis, February 14, 19, March 3, 1874, Davis to Overton, February 19, 1874 – all in Governor's Papers.

[23]*St. Paul Daily Pioneer*, March 14, 1874.

[24]Warren Upham and Rose B. Dunlap, *Minnesota Biographies*, 115, 167, 381 (*Minnesota Historical Collections*, vol. 14, 1912); James H. Baker, *Lives of the Governors of Minnesota*, 129–144 (*Minnesota Historical Collections*, vol. 13, 1908); G. C. Chamberlin to Davis, February 17, 1874, Governor's Papers.

[25]Here and below, see Minutes of Meeting, Seed Wheat Commissioners, March 17, 1874, Governor's Papers.

[26]*St. Paul Daily Pioneer*, March 25, 1874.

[27]Samuel Truax, Jacob Rouse, John W. Blake, "Seed Wheat Distribution," April 3, 1874, Governor's Papers.

[28]Sibley to Davis, April 8, 14, 1874, Governor's Papers.

[29]Davis sent the same letter to fourteen men from throughout southwestern Minnesota. Davis to Edward Savage *et al.*, May 18, Savage to Davis, May 19, John T. Smith to Davis, May 20, George Thompson to Davis, May 19, William Bird, Jr., to Davis, May 21, Daniel Rohrer to Davis, May 21, Leonard Aldrich to Davis, June 3 – all 1874, in Governor's Papers.

[30]*Senate Journal*, 1875, p. 97–99.

[31]Letter reprinted in Rose, *History of Jackson County*, 149; *Martin County Sentinel*, July 10, 1874; George I. Parsons to Sibley, March 18, Warren Smith to Sibley, March 18, "Final Report of Relief Committee," June 27 – all 1874, in Sibley Papers;

Minutes of Meetings, March 20, 28, 1874, April 20, 1875, Minnehaha Grange Papers, DAM-MHS; Minutes of Meetings, April 5, 18, July 18, November 21, December 5, 1874, North Star Grange Papers, DAM-MHS.

[32] Here and below, see *St. Paul Daily Pioneer*, July 4, 1874; Solon Justus Buck, *The Granger Movement: A Study of Agricultural Organization and Its Political, Economic and Social Manifestations, 1870–1880*, 283, 284 (Cambridge, Mass., 1913). On the political strength of the Minnesota Grange, see D. Sven Nordin, *Rich Harvest: A History of the Grange, 1867–1900*, 169–173 (Jackson, Miss., 1974).

[33] Clear Lake Grange to Sibley, July 13, 1874, Granite Falls Grange to Davis, July 19, 1874 – both in Governor's Papers. See also other letters to Davis from various Granges throughout the state in the Governor's Papers.

[34] Charles M. Gardner, *The Grange — Friend of the Farmer: A Concise Reference History of America's Oldest Farm Organization, and the Only Rural Fraternity in the World, 1867–1947*, 46, 240 (Washington, D.C., 1949); Nordin, *Rich Harvest*, 128.

[35] *Senate Journal*, 1875, p. 99, 100.

[36] *St. Paul Daily Pioneer*, July 7, 1874.

[37] *St. Paul Daily Pioneer*, July 14, 1874; *Senate Journal*, 1875, p. 97, 98; Wright County Auditor to Davis, July 31, Francis Bassan to Davis, July [?], F. X. Goulet to Davis, July 13 – all 1874, in Governor's Papers. See also *Martin County Sentinel*, August 14, 1874.

[38] Here and below, see Upham and Dunlap, *Minnesota Biographies*, 25, 177, 349, 603; *Senate Journal*, 1875, p. 97–99.

[39] *Senate Journal*, 1875, p. 101, 102.

[40] Joshua Swan to Davis, July 20, 1874, Henry B. Whipple to Davis, August 1, 1874 – both in Governor's Papers; *Senate Journal*, 1875, p. 102–104.

[41] *Senate Journal*, 1875, p. 98, 102.

[42] *St. Paul Daily Pioneer*, January 27, 1875.

[43] Minnesota, *Laws*, 1875, p. 182.

[44] Minnesota, *Laws*, 1875, p. 46, 48.

[45] Minnesota, *Laws*, 1875, p. 183.

[46] Cushman K. Davis, "Annual Message," January 7, 1876, in Minnesota, *Executive Documents*, 1875, p. 34; Edward F. Wade to Davis, March 15, William H. Rich to Davis, February 11, Hans Knudson to Davis, March 2 – all 1875, in Governor's Papers.

[47] Renville County Commissioners to Davis, [March, 1875], Governor's Papers; Rose, *Counties of Rock and Pipestone*, 83.

[48] Martin County Relief Receipts, 1875, Governor's Papers; U.S. Manuscript Census Schedules, 1870 and 1880, Martin County, microfilm copy in DAM-MHS.

[49] Davis, "Annual Message," January 7, 1876, p. 33; *Martin County Sentinel*, April 9, May 14, 1875; Rose, *Nobles County*, 88; *St. Paul Daily Pioneer*, March 28, 1875.

[50] Davis, "Annual Message," January 7, 1876, p. 33; [Wise, Smith, and Whitman], *The Grasshopper*.

Chapter 6. *Governor Pillsbury's Response*

[1] Baker, *Lives of the Governors*, 232; Betty Kane, "The 1876 Legislature: A Case Study in Lively Futility," in *Minnesota History*, 45:223–240 (Summer, 1977); Blegen, *Minnesota*, 294 (quotation).

[2] Kane, in *Minnesota History*, 45:225; John S. Pillsbury, "Inaugural Message," January 7, 1876, in Minnesota, *Executive Documents*, 1875, p. 3–28 (quotations, 6).

[3]Proclamation of Governor John S. Pillsbury, August 30, 1876, *Executive Record*, vol. E, 528–530, Governor's Papers.

[4]John S. Pillsbury, "Annual Message," January 4, 1877, in Minnesota, *Executive Documents*, 1876, p. 38, 39.

[5]Bremner, *The Public Good*, 201, 202.

[6]Here and below, see Baker, *Lives of the Governors*, 225–250; [Joseph A. A. Burnquist], *Minnesota and Its People*, 3:5 (Chicago, 1924).

[7]*St. Paul Daily Pioneer Press*, March 9, 1876, May 31, 1877.

[8]*St. Paul Daily Pioneer Press*, February 2, 1877.

[9]*Worthington Western Advance*, July 11, 1874; *Martin County Sentinel*, July 11, 1874; *Pioneer Press* (St. Paul and Minneapolis), November 1, 1876; Joseph Flanders to Davis, August 15, 1874, Governor's Papers.

[10]Proclamation of Governor Pillsbury, August 30, 1876, *Executive Record*, vol. E, 528–530, Governor's Papers.

[11]Pillsbury, "Annual Message," January 4, 1877, p. 38, 39.

[12]Proclamation of Governor Pillsbury, August 30, 1876, *Executive Record*, vol. E, 528, Governor's Papers; *The Rocky Mountain Locust, or Grasshopper, being the Report of Proceedings of a Conference of the Governors of Several Western States and Territories*, 19–58 (St. Louis, 1876).

[13]Proclamation of Governor Pillsbury, August 30, 1876, *Executive Record*, vol. E, 529, Governor's Papers; Pillsbury, "Annual Message," January 4, 1877, p. 39.

[14]Pillsbury, "Annual Message," January 4, 1877, p. 39.

[15]*St. Paul Pioneer Press*, January 14, 1877.

[16]Philip W. Pillsbury, *The Pioneering Pillsburys*, 17 (New York, 1950).

[17]Pillsbury, "Annual Message," January 4, 1877, p. 39.

[18]Here and below, see *St. Paul Pioneer Press*, January 4, 1877.

[19]*St. Paul Pioneer Press*, February 2, 1877.

[20]*St. Paul Pioneer Press*, January 20, 1877; McClure, *More Than a Roof*, 55; Upham and Dunlap, *Minnesota Biographies*, 603.

[21]*St. Paul Pioneer Press*, January 5, 11, 13, February 1, 1877.

[22]*St. Paul Pioneer Press*, January 30, February 2, 3, 1877.

[23]*St. Paul Pioneer Press*, February 6, 1877.

[24]*St. Paul Pioneer Press*, December 27, 1876.

[25]E. Julius Hielscher, September 16, 1876, Norman Pitney to Pillsbury, March 5, John N. Hall to Pillsbury, March 8, David R. Breed to Pillsbury, March 8, David R. Noyes to Pillsbury, March 20, D. A. Dickinson to Pillsbury, March 20, S. N. Sherwin to Pillsbury, March 20, J. C. Noe to Pillsbury, March 21, Worthington Citizens to Pillsbury, April 9 — all 1877, in Governor's Papers; *St. Paul Pioneer Press*, March 30, 31, April 1, 25, 26, 10, May 18, 1877; Proclamation of Governor John S. Pillsbury, April 9, 1877, *Executive Record*, vol. F, 18, Governor's Papers; Breed, *Locust-Scourge*, 7, 8.

[26]*St. Paul Pioneer Press*, November 21, 25, 29, 1877; "Help for the Grasshopper Sufferers" and "Suggestions to Collectors," Broadside Collection, DAM-MHS.

[27]*St. Paul Pioneer Press*, May 25, 26, 29, 30, 1877; State Auditor, *Reports*, 1878, p. 255; O. C. Gregg to Pillsbury, May 29, Leonard Aldrich to Pillsbury, May 29, William Tubbs to Pillsbury, May 29, H. S. Sjoberg to Pillsbury, May 31 — all 1877, in Governor's Papers; Minnesota, *Laws*, 1878, p. 177.

[28]John S. Pillsbury, "Annual Message," January 11, 1878, in Minnesota, *Executive Documents*, 1877, p. 44, 45.

[29]*Pioneer Press and Tribune* (St. Paul and Minneapolis), June 21, 1876.

Chapter 7. *The "Cold Charity" of the State*

[1] [Wise, Smith, and Whitman], *The Grasshopper*, 45–47.

[2] *St. Paul Daily Pioneer Press*, January 19, 1876; *House Journal*, 1876, p. 293, 294, 386.

[3] Minnesota, *Laws*, 1876, p. 116, 140; Thomas Hughes, *History of Blue Earth County and Biographies of Its Leading Citizens*, 183, 184 (Chicago, [1909?]); [Wise, Smith, and Whitman], *The Grasshopper*, 45; *St. Paul Daily Pioneer Press*, January 22, 1876.

[4] Minnesota, *Laws*, 1876, p. 113, 140, 153, *Special Laws*, 1876, p. 260.

[5] Kane, in *Minnesota History*, 45:223–240; Walter N. Trenerry, "The Minnesota Legislator and the Grasshopper, 1873–77," in *Minnesota History*, 36:54–61 (June, 1958).

[6] *Senate Journal*, 1877, p. 7, 14, 23, 25; *St. Paul Daily Pioneer Press*, January 6, 11, 1877; Minnesota, *Laws*, 1877, p. 177.

[7] Minnesota, *Laws*, 1877, p. 243, 280–282; *Senate Journal*, 1877, p. 43.

[8] Minnesota, *Laws*, 1877, p. 205, 234.

[9] Minnesota, *Laws*, 1877, p. 69, 173, 174.

[10] Here and two paragraphs below, see *St. Paul Daily Pioneer Press*, January 9, 1877; *Senate Journal*, 1877, p. 193, 194, 252; Minnesota, *Laws*, 1877, p. 246–248.

[11] Appropriation of 1877, for Seed Grain for Grasshopper Sufferers, Martin County, March 12, 1877, Governor's Papers; Commissioner of Statistics, *Reports*, 1878, p. 66; *St. Paul Daily Pioneer Press*, March 16, 27, 1877. See also the county lists of applicants in the Governor's Papers. In March 1877, when the seed was purchased, wheat sold for about $1.25 per bushel. After harvest, it brought about $.80 per bushel. Rose, *Counties of Rock and Pipestone*, 89, 90.

[12] *St. Paul Daily Pioneer Press*, February 18, March 11, 21, 29, 1877.

[13] Here and below, see *St. Paul Daily Pioneer Press*, March 21, 1877.

[14] Minnesota, *Laws*, 1877, p. 171–174.

[15] *St. Paul Daily Pioneer Press*, February 8, 1877.

[16] *St. Paul Daily Pioneer Press*, February 16, 1877; Pillsbury, "Annual Message," January 11, 1878, p. 43; Minnesota, *Laws*, 1877, p. 174.

[17] There are well over 100 letters or petitions of nominations for measurers in the Governor's Papers.

[18] J. B. Wakefield to Pillsbury, March 21, W. W. White and F. W. Temple to Pillsbury, [May], Nicollet County Citizens to Pillsbury, [May], Shelby and Pleasant Mound Granges to Pillsbury, May 8, D. S. McGraw to Pillsbury, May 1, J. A. Armstrong to Pillsbury, May 2 — all 1877, in Governor's Papers.

[19] Petition from Meeker County, undated, Meeker County Residents to Pillsbury, April 30, Hamler Stevens to Pillsbury, May 2, E. Evanson to Pillsbury, June 2, E. A. D. Salter to Pillsbury, May 28, Spicer Larson to Pillsbury, May 31 — all 1877, in Governor's Papers; *St. Paul Daily Pioneer Press*, May 31, 1877.

[20] Pillsbury, "Annual Message," January 11, 1878, p. 43; *St. Paul Daily Pioneer Press*, May 31, 1877; Kiester, *History of Faribault County*, 441.

[21] *House Journal*, 1878, p. 8; Minnesota, *Laws*, 1878, p. 125–128, 157, 174.

[22] Apportionment to Counties, Report of Seed Grain Distribution 1878, and Seed Grain Records, Martin, Watonwan, and Redwood counties — both in Governor's Papers; Seed Grain Record, Chippewa County, Chippewa County Courthouse, Montevideo; State Auditor, *Reports*, 1890, p. 293, 346.

Chapter 8. *The Federal Government's Role*

[1]Bremner, *American Philanthropy*, 89–104.

[2]Josephine Chaplin Brown, *Federal Unemployment Relief, 1929–1939*, 21–24, 37 (New York, 1940); Walter I. Trattner, "The Federal Government and Social Welfare in Early Nineteenth-Century America," in *Social Service Review*, 50:243–255 (June, 1976).

[3]June Axinn and Herman Levin, *Social Welfare: A History of the American Response to Need*, 37 (New York, 1975); Woodruffe, *From Charity to Social Work*, 156; Leiby, *History of Social Welfare*, 104; Trattner, in *Social Service Review*, 50:231, 232.

[4]Axinn and Levin, *Social Welfare*, 105.

[5]Here and below, see 73 Congress, 1 session, *Hearings on Relief Legislation, United States Senate, February 3, 1933*, part 2, p. 547–550 (Washington, D.C., 1933).

[6]Minnesota, *Laws*, 1874, p. 286.

[7]*Congressional Record*, 43 Congress, 1 session, 4595; *Worthington Western Advance*, June 6, 1874; United States, *Statutes at Large*, 43:1:308, 43:2:10, 44:1:104, 44:1:134, 44:2:127, 45:2:314.

[8]Register of (Initial) Homestead Entries, General Land Office Papers.

[9]Here and below, see *St. Paul Daily Pioneer Press*, January 4, 1877.

[10]U.S., *Statutes at Large*, 44:1:102, 45:2:190; *Martin County Sentinel*, September 4, 1874.

[11]U.S., *Statutes at Large*, 43:2:25; Frederick Watts to Davis, February 10, Mark Dunnell to Davis, February 25, Report of seeds received & issued by the Seed Grain Commissioners for and in behalf of the U.S. Agricultural Department (donated), Watts to Davis, March 23 – all 1875, in Governor's Papers; *Martin County Sentinel*, March 26, 1875; U.S. Commissioner of Agriculture, *Report*, 1875, p. 13, 14.

[12]*Congressional Record*, 44 Congress, 2 session, 1757, 1758; *St. Paul Daily Pioneer Press* (quoting *Glencoe Register*), April 21, 1877.

[13]*St. Paul Daily Pioneer Press*, February 21, 1878.

[14]Sidney Dillon to William Belknap, September 26, 1874, Meigs to Belknap, September 28, 1874, Belknap to Dillon, September 29, 1874, Consolidated File, Records of the Office of the Quartermaster General – all National Archives Record Group 92 (hereafter cited as NARG).

[15]Cincinnati (Ohio) Chamber of Commerce to Belknap, October 3, 1874, C. G. Finney to Ulysses S. Grant, forwarded to War Department, June 3, 1875 – both in Letters Received, Records of the Office of the Secretary of War, NARG 107; Adjutant General to War Department, November 6, 1874, Consolidated File, Records of the Office of the Quartermaster General, NARG 92.

[16]Robert N. Manley, "In the Wake of the Grasshoppers: Public Relief in Nebraska, 1874–1875," in *Nebraska History*, 44:255–275 (December, 1963); Gilbert C. Fite, "The United States Army and Relief to Pioneer Settlers, 1874–1875," in *Journal of the West*, 6:99–107 (January, 1967); Gary D. Olson, ed., "Relief for Nebraska Grasshopper Victims: The Official Journal of Lieutenant Theodore E. True," in *Minnesota History*, 48:119–140 (Summer, 1967).

[17]Here and three paragraphs below, see 43 Congress, 2 session, *Senate Executive Documents*, no. 5, p. 4, 5, 8 (serial 1629). The Military Division of the Missouri included the Departments of the Dakota (Minnesota and Dakota Territory), the Platte (Nebraska and Iowa), and the Missouri (Kansas and Colorado).

[18]Ulysses S. Grant to Secretary of War, November 12, 1874, Letters Received, Records of the Office of the Secretary of War, NARG 107; Adjutant General to E. O. C. Ord, November 16, 1874, Letters Sent, Records of the Office of the Adjutant General, NARG 94.

[19]Adjutant General to P. H. Sheridan, November 30, 1874, Letters Sent, Records of the Office of the Adjutant General, NARG 94.

[20] *Congressional Record*, 43 Congress, 1 session, 3171, 3172; Paul H. Hutton, "Philip H. Sheridan and the Army of the West," 17, Ph.D. thesis, Indiana University, 1980.

[21] Ord to Belknap, December 19, 1874, P. W. Hitchcock to Belknap, December 15, 17, 1874, Letters Received, Records of the Office of the Secretary of War, NARG 107; Belknap to Secretary of Senate, December 21, 1874, 43 Congress, 2 session, *Senate Executive Documents*, no. 5, p. 1 (serial 1629).

[22] Adjutant General to Ord, January 6, 1875, Letters Sent, Records of the Office of the Adjutant General, NARG 94.

[23] Here and below, see *Congressional Record*, 43 Congress, 2 session, 887, 888, 969; U.S., *Statutes at Large*, 43:2:40.

[24] *Martin County Sentinel*, December 4, 1874.

[25] Alfred Terry to Davis, February 16, 1875, Assistant Adjutant General to H. S. Howe, *et al.*, February 21, 1875, Letters Sent, Department of Dakota, Papers of the United States Army Continental Commands, NARG 393.

[26] Assistant Adjutant General to J. M. Burns, March 1, Assistant Adjutant General to M. W. Keogh, March 9, Alfred Terry to Assistant Adjutant General, Military Division of the Missouri, March 26, 30 — all 1875, Letters Sent, Department of Dakota, Papers of the U.S. Army Continental Commands, NARG 393; 44 Congress, 1 session, *House Executive Documents*, no. 1, part 2, p. 68 (serial 1674).

[27] *St. Paul Daily Pioneer*, March 12, 27, 1875.

[28] 44 Congress, 1 session, *House Executive Documents*, no. 1, part 2, p. 69 (serial 1674); *St. Paul Daily Pioneer*, December 1, 1875.

[29] Warren Smith to Sibley, April 7, Charles Wagner to Davis, April 21, William M. Bear to Davis, April 29, T. S. Curtis to Davis, May 5 — all 1875, in Governor's Papers.

[30] John Wiggins to Davis, March 24, Thomas Clipperton to S. P. Henneson, forwarded to Davis, May 26 — both 1875, in Governor's Papers.

[31] Here and two paragraphs below, see 44 Congress, 1 session, *House Executive Documents*, no. 28, p. 19, 20 (serial 1687).

[32] Belknap to Ord, March 11, 1875, Letters Sent, Records of the Office of the Adjutant General, NARG 94.

[33] *Rocky Mountain Locust, or Grasshopper*, 2, 3, 6.

[34] *Rocky Mountain Locust, or Grasshopper*, 22.

[35] Cyrus Thomas to Ferdinand V. Hayden, October 4, 1872, A. S. Packard to Hayden, March 10, 1876, Charles V. Riley to Hayden, January 6, 1876, Thomas to Hayden, March 18, 1876, Letters Received, Geological and Geographical Survey of the Territories, 1872–79, NARG 57.

[36] Thomas to Hayden, March 18, 1876, Packard to Hayden, October 25, 1876, Letters Received, Geological and Geographical Survey of the Territories, 1872–79, NARG 57.

[37] Thomas to Hayden, October 28, 1876, Letters Received, Geological and Geographical Survey of the Territories, 1872–79, NARG 57; U.S., *Statutes at Large*, 44:2:105; Riley to Pillsbury, April 6, 1877, Governor's Papers; A. G. Porter to Carl Schurz, June 27, 1879, Papers of the United States Entomological Commission, Records of the Interior Dept., NARG 48.

[38] U.S. Dept. of the Interior, *Bulletin of the United States Entomological Commission*, No. 1, *Destruction of the Young or Unfledged Locust* (Washington, D.C., 1877), No. 2, *On the Natural History of the Rocky Mountain Locust, and on the Habits of the Young or Unfledged Insects as They Occur in the More Fertile Country in Which They Will Hatch the Present Year* (Washington, D.C., 1877); U.S. Geological Survey, *Report, 1877*; U.S. Dept. of the Interior, Geological Survey, *Report, 1878, 1879* (Washington, D.C., 1880).

Index

INDEX

U.S. Dept. of Agriculture, distributes seed, 111; entomology criticized, 122–123

U.S. Dept. of War, involvement in relief, 112–121

U.S. Entomological Commission, estimates grasshopper damages, 13, 15; established, 122; work, 123

U.S. Geological and Geographic Survey of the Territories, 122, 123

U.S. Signal Corps, grasshopper research, 123

Utah, grasshoppers, 13

VEGETABLES, crop losses, 23, 35, 36

WADE, EDWARD F., relief work, 53–56

Washington, grasshoppers, 13

Watonwan County, population, 33; county relief, 51; state relief, 87, 104

Weather, impact on grasshoppers, 24, 27; winter, 56; disasters, 58; drought, 105

West Cedar Township, Martin County, relief, 53–56

Wheat, annual losses, 21, 23, 24, 26, 29, 56; harvest, 29; acreage, 39; in seed-grain relief, 72, 104, 111. *See also* Grain

Wilder, Laura Ingalls, novelist, 17; family, 33, 35

Windom, William, U.S. senator, 109

Winona, relief contributions, 60, 91–92

Winona County, relief contribution, 60

Wisconsin, aid solicited, 50

Work ethic, as an American value, 8–12, 31, 124; relation to relief, 42, 43, 84, 95

Worthington, land office, 34

Worthington Western Advance, criticizes relief, 87

Wright County, aid solicited, 76

Wyoming, grasshoppers, 13

YOUNG MEN'S CHRISTIAN ASSN., 45